Themes
for Today

1

Third Edition

Reading for Today SERIES, BOOK 1

LORRAINE C. SMITH

AND

NANCY NICI MARE

English Language Institute
Queens College
The City University of New York

HEINLE
CENGAGE Learning

Australia • Brazil • Japan • Korea • Mexico • Singapore • Spain • United Kingdom • United States

HEINLE
CENGAGE Learning

**Reading for Today 1: Themes for Today
Third Edition**
Lorraine C. Smith and Nancy Nici Mare

Publisher, the Americas, Global, and
Dictionaries: Sherrise Roehr

Acquisitions Editor: Thomas Jefferies

Senior Development Editor:
Laura Le Dréan

Senior Content Project Manager:
Maryellen E. Killeen

Director of US Marketing:
James McDonough

Senior Product Marketing Manager:
Katie Kelley

Academic Marketing Manager:
Caitlin Driscoll

Director of Global Marketing: Ian Martin

Senior Print Buyer: Betsy Donaghey

Compositor: PreMediaGlobal

Cover and Interior Design: Muse Group

Printer: RR Donnelley

Library of Congress Control Number: 2010929133

ISBN-13: 978-1-111-03358-3

ISBN-10: 1-111-03358-7

Heinle
20 Channel Center Street
Boston, MA 02210
USA

Cengage Learning is a leading provider of customized learning solutions
with office locations around the globe, including Singapore, the United
Kingdom, Australia, Mexico, Brazil, and Japan. Locate your local office at
international.cengage.com/region

Cengage Learning products are represented in Canada by
Nelson Education, Ltd.

Visit Heinle online at **elt.heinle.com**

Visit our corporate website at **www.cengage.com**

Printed in Canada
1 2 3 4 5 6 7 8 9 14 13 12 11 10

To Tom

CREDITS

CONTENTS

Skills Chart   vii
Preface   x
Introduction   xiii
Acknowledgments   xvi

UNIT 1   Language and Culture   1

Chapter 1   **Learning a Second Language**   2
It is not always easy to learn a second language, but there are some ways to make learning one a little easier.

Chapter 2   **The Best Place to Live**   17
What is the best place to live? Most Americans are happy in their hometown. However, some people want to move to a different place.

UNIT 2   Home and Family   35

Chapter 3   **The McCaugheys: An Unusual Family**   36
Bobbi and Ken McCaughey have a very large family. They have septuplets—seven children born together—and an older child, too!

Chapter 4   **A Musical Family**   49
This family moved away from the city to start a new life. Now the parents and their children play musical instruments together instead of video games.

UNIT 3   Exercise and Fitness   63

Chapter 5   **The Importance of Exercise for Children**   64
Children need a lot of exercise. It is very important for their health. However, in some schools, children do not get exercise every day.

Chapter 6   **The New York City Marathon: A World Race**   78
The New York City Marathon is very popular. People come from many different countries all around the world to run together.

UNIT 4 Remarkable Researchers 93

Chapter 7 **Margaret Mead: The World Was Her Home** 94
This famous anthropologist loved to learn about different cultures. She also wrote books so that other people could learn about them, too.

Chapter 8 **Louis Pasteur: A Modern-Day Scientist** 107
This important scientist made many discoveries to help people stay healthy. These important discoveries are still useful and necessary today.

UNIT 5 Science and History 123

Chapter 9 **The Origin of the Moon** 124
People have many questions about the moon, for example, "Where did it come from?" Scientists have some theories to help answer these questions.

Chapter 10 **A New Route across the Top of the World** 139
The Northeast Passage, which connects the Atlantic Ocean and the Pacific Ocean, is not covered in ice all year anymore. Now ships can travel between Europe and Asia much more quickly.

UNIT 6 Future Technology Today 155

Chapter 11 **Saving Lives with Weather Forecasting** 156
Tornadoes can be very dangerous. New kinds of weather technology can help predict when a tornado will occur. This can help save lives, too.

Chapter 12 **Clues and Criminal Investigation** 172
Crime experts look for different kinds of evidence at a crime scene. These clues help them to find criminals and to solve crimes.

Index of Key Words and Phrases 189
Skills Index 191

SKILLS

UNIT Chapter and Title	Reading Skills Focus	Structure Focus	Follow-up Activities Skills Focus
Unit 1 **Language and Culture** *Page 1* **Chapter 1** **Learning a Second Language** *Page 2*	• Preview a reading • Use a chart to list ideas • Understand *True / False*, Multiple Choice, and Short Answer questions • Scan for information • Recall information • Identify main idea • Use context clues • Understand vocabulary from context • Recognize word partners	• Identify parts of speech: adjectives and adverbs • Recognize the suffix *-ly*	• *Discussion:* Ask for and give suggestions • *Writing:* Write a list; write a letter; write a journal entry
Chapter 2 **The Best Place to Live** *Page 17*	• Preview a reading • Use the title to predict content • Understand *True / False*, Multiple Choice, and Short Answer questions • Scan for information • Understand vocabulary in context • Identify main ideas and details • Use context clues • Make inferences • Recognize word partners • Interpret pie charts	• Identify parts of speech: adjectives and nouns • Recognize the suffix *-ness*	• *Discussion:* Give reasons; talk about charts • *Writing:* Write a paragraph with reasons; write a journal entry
Unit 2 **Home and Family** *Page 35* **Chapter 3** **The McCaugheys: An Unusual Family** *Page 36*	• Preview a reading • Understand *True / False*, Multiple Choice, and Short Answer questions • Scan for information • Predict content • Use context clues • Understand vocabulary from context • Identify main idea • Draw conclusions • Recognize word partners	• Identify parts of speech: nouns and verbs	• *Discussion:* Talk about a schedule; ask interview questions • *Writing:* Write a schedule; write an opinion paragraph; write a journal entry
Chapter 4 **A Musical Family** *Page 49*	• Preview a reading • Use title and visuals to predict content • Understand *True / False*, Multiple Choice, and Short Answer questions • Understand main ideas • Scan for information • Understand vocabulary from context • Draw conclusions • Recognize word partners	• Identify parts of speech: nouns and verbs	• *Discussion:* Give an opinion; listen and note opinions of others • *Writing:* Write a descriptive paragraph; write a journal entry
Unit 3 **Exercise and Fitness** *Page 63* **Chapter 5** **The Importance of Exercise for Children** *Page 64*	• Use the title to predict content • Use visuals to preview a reading • Understand *True / False*, Multiple Choice, and Short Answer questions • Scan for information • Make inferences • Understand transitional words and phrases • Understand vocabulary from context • Identify the main idea • Recognize word partners	• Identify parts of speech: nouns and verbs	• *Discussion:* Discuss an exercise plan; categorize activities; make suggestions • *Writing:* Write a letter; write a paragraph with reasons; write a journal entry

UNIT Chapter and Title	Reading Skills Focus	Structure Focus	Follow-up Activities Skills Focus
Chapter 6 **The New York City Marathon:** **A World Race** *Page 78*	• Use visuals and the title to preview a reading • Make predictions • Understand *True / False*, Multiple Choice, and Short Answer questions • Scan for information • Read for supporting details • Understand vocabulary in context • Interpret numerical information on a graph • Recognize word partners	• Identify parts of speech: nouns and verbs • Recognize the suffix *-ment*	• *Discussion:* Talk about a process; give advice; talk about a graph • *Writing:* Make a list of suggestions; write a letter; write a journal entry
Unit 4 **Remarkable Researchers** *Page 93* **Chapter 7** **Margaret Mead: The World** **Was Her Home** *Page 94*	• Preview a chapter using visuals and the title • Predict content • Identify the main idea • Understand *True / False*, Multiple Choice, and Short Answer questions • Scan for information • Understand vocabulary in context • Recognize word partners	• Identify parts of speech: nouns and verbs • Recognize the suffixes *-ence* and *-ance*	• *Discussion:* Interview others about their culture; discuss interview findings • *Writing:* Write a descriptive paragraph; write a journal entry
Chapter 8 **Louis Pasteur: A Modern-Day** **Scientist** *Page 107*	• Preview a chapter using visuals and the title • Understand *True / False*, Multiple Choice, and Short Answer questions • Understand vocabulary from context • Scan for supporting details • Recognize word partners	• Identify parts of speech: nouns and verbs • Recognize the suffix *-tion*	• *Discussion:* Give opinions; discuss and compare academic interests • *Writing:* Write an expository paragraph; use supporting examples; write a journal entry
Unit 5 **Science and History** *Page 123* **Chapter 9** **The Origin of the Moon** *Page 124*	• Use background knowledge to preview content • Understand *True / False*, Multiple Choice, and Short Answer questions • Scan for information • Understand vocabulary in context • Make inferences • Recognize word partners	• Identify parts of speech: nouns and verbs • Recognize the suffix *-tion*	• *Discussion:* Create a plan; compare ideas; evaluate plans • *Writing:* Make a list; write an opinion paragraph; write a letter; write a journal entry
Chapter 10 **A New Route across the Top** **of the World** *Page 139*	• Preview a chapter using visuals and the title • Understand *True / False*, Multiple Choice, and Short Answer questions • Scan for information • Understand vocabulary from context • Look at art and maps to help comprehension • Understand content area vocabulary: maps and measurement • Recognize word partners • Interpret maps	• Identify parts of speech: nouns and verbs	• *Discussion:* Make and compare lists • *Writing:* Write a paragraph with reasons; write a journal entry

SKILLS

UNIT Chapter and Title	Reading Skills Focus	Structure Focus	Follow-up Activities Skills Focus
Unit 6 **Future Technology Today** *Page 155* **Chapter 11** **Saving Lives with Weather Forecasting** *Page 156*	• Use visuals and the title to preview a reading • Predict content • Understand *True / False*, Multiple Choice, and Short Answer questions • Understand vocabulary from context • Identify main ideas • Scan for details • Understand content area vocabulary: weather • Answer open-ended questions • Sequence events • Interpret charts • Recognize word partners	• Identify parts of speech: nouns and verbs • Recognize the suffixes *-ence* and *-ance*	• *Discussion:* Talk about a process; compare ideas • *Writing:* Write a paragraph with reasons; write a descriptive paragraph; write a journal entry
Chapter 12 **Clues and Criminal Investigation** *Page 172*	• Preview vocabulary • Use the title to predict content • Understand *True / False*, Multiple Choice, and Short Answer questions • Scan for information • Understand content area vocabulary: crime and forensics • Understand vocabulary from context • Identify main ideas • Find supporting details and examples • Recognize word partners	• Identify parts of speech: nouns and adjectives • Recognize the suffix *-ful*	• *Discussion:* Solve problems; compare solutions; evaluate solutions; retell a news story • *Writing:* Write a descriptive paragraph; write an opinion paragraph; write a journal entry
	• **Index of Key Words and Phrases** *Page 189* • **Skills Index** *Page 191*		

PREFACE

Themes for Today, Third Edition is a reading skills text intended for beginning English-as-a-second or foreign-language (ESL/EFL) students. The topics in this text are fresh and timely, and the book has a strong global focus.

Themes for Today is one in a series of five reading skills texts. The complete series, *Reading for Today*, has been designed to meet the needs of students from the beginning to the advanced levels and includes the following:

- *Reading for Today 1: Themes for Today*   beginning
- *Reading for Today 2: Insights for Today*   high beginning
- *Reading for Today 3: Issues for Today*   intermediate
- *Reading for Today 4: Concepts for Today*   high intermediate
- *Reading for Today 5: Topics for Today*   advanced

Themes for Today, Third Edition provides students with essential practice in the types of reading skills they will need in an academic environment. It requires students not only to read text but also to extract basic information from various kinds of charts, graphs, illustrations, and photographs. Beginning-level students are rarely exposed to this type of reading material. Furthermore, students are given the opportunity to speak and write about their own cultures and compare their experiences with those of students from other countries. The text also includes activities that encourage students to go outside the classroom. These tasks provide students with opportunities to practice reading, writing, speaking, and listening to English in the real world. Thus, all four skills are incorporated into each chapter.

Themes for Today, Third Edition has been designed for flexible use by teachers and students. The text consists of six units. Each unit contains two chapters that deal with related topics. At the same time, though, each chapter is entirely separate in content from the other chapter in that unit. This gives the instructor the option of either completing entire units or choosing individual chapters as a focus in class. Although the chapters are organized by level of difficulty, the teacher and students may choose to work with the chapters out of order, depending on available time and the interests of the class. The activities and exercises in each chapter have been organized to flow from general comprehension, including main ideas and supporting details, through vocabulary in context, to critical thinking skills. However, the teacher may choose to work on the exercises in any order, depending on time and on the students' abilities.

Readers, especially beginning second language readers, vary considerably in their strategy use and comprehension monitoring activities. Some readers benefit more from focusing on reading one or two paragraphs at a time and checking their comprehension before continuing to read. Other readers may prefer to read an entire passage and then consider questions related to the reading. Consequently, in order to provide maximum flexibility, all the reading passages are presented in two formats: (1) in sections and (2) in their complete form. When the reading is presented in sections, each segment is followed by questions on content and vocabulary. Where the reading is presented in its complete form, it is followed by questions on content that ask the reader for inferences, conclusions, opinions, and main ideas. With this dual format, the teacher and students have three choices: all the students may read the passage in segments, then read it in its entirety; all the students may read the passage completely first, then attend to the questions following each segment; or the students may each choose which format they prefer to read first, according to their own preferences and needs.

The exercises that follow the reading passages are carefully crafted to help students develop and improve vocabulary, reading proficiency, and comprehension of English sentence structure.

Lower-level language students need considerable visual reinforcement of ideas and vocabulary. Therefore, this text contains many illustrations. In addition, many of the follow-up activities enable students to manipulate the information in the text. The teacher may want the students to use the board to work on the charts and lists in the activities throughout the chapters.

Much of the vocabulary is recycled in the exercises and activities in any given chapter, as well as throughout the book. Experience has shown that beginning-level students especially need repeated exposure to new vocabulary and word forms. Repetition of vocabulary in varied contexts helps the students not only understand the new vocabulary better, but also remember it.

As students work through the text, they will improve their reading skills and develop confidence in their growing English proficiency. At the same time, the teacher will be notice the students' steady progress towards skillful, independent reading.

New to the Third Edition

The third edition of *Themes for Today* maintains the effective approach of the second edition with several significant improvements.

The third edition of *Themes for Today* contains two completely new chapters: *The Best Place to Live* in the Language and Culture unit and *A New Route across the Top of the World* in the Science and History unit. In addition, the third edition includes new photos and updated information, graphs and charts, all of which are designed to enhance students' comprehension of the readings. The *Topics for Discussion and Writing* section has been expanded as well to give students the opportunity to answer questions that are not only interesting and thought-provoking, but also relevant.

These enhancements to *Themes for Today, Third Edition* have been made to help students improve their reading skills, to reinforce vocabulary, and to encourage interest in the topics. These skills are intended to prepare students for academic work and the technical world of information they are about to encounter.

How to Use This Book

Every chapter in this book consists of the following:

- Prereading Preparation
- Reading Passage in Segments with Reading Analysis
- Complete Reading Passage
- Scanning for Information
- Word Forms
- Word Partnership Box
- Vocabulary in Context
- Topics for Discussion and Writing
- Follow-up Activities
- Crossword Puzzle
- Cloze Quiz

There is also an *Index of Key Words and Phrases* at the end of the book.

The format of each chapter in the book is consistent. Although each chapter can be done entirely in class, some exercises may be assigned for homework. This, of course, depends on the individual teacher's preference as well as the availability of class time. Class work will be most effective when done in pairs or groups, giving the students more opportunity to interact with the material and with each other.

Prereading Preparation

This prereading activity is designed to stimulate student interest and provide preliminary vocabulary for the passage itself. The importance of prereading preparation should not be underestimated. Studies have shown the positive effect of prereading preparation in motivating students and in enhancing reading comprehension. In fact, prereading discussion of topics and visuals has been shown to be more effective in improving reading comprehension than prereading vocabulary exercises per se. Time should be spent describing and discussing the illustrations as well as discussing the prereading questions. Furthermore, students should try to relate the topics to their own experience and try to predict what they are going to read about. Students may even choose to write a story based on the chapter-opening illustration.

Reading Passage in Segments

Each reading passage is presented in segments. As the students read the passage for the first time, they can focus on the meaning of each paragraph. The reading analysis questions that follow each segment require the students to think about the meanings of words and phrases, the structure of sentences and paragraphs, and the relationships of ideas to each other. Students also have the opportunity to think about and predict what they will read in the next section of the reading. These exercises are very effective when done in groups. They may also be done individually, but groups give the students an opportunity to discuss possible answers.

Reading Passage

Students should be instructed to read the entire passage carefully a second time and to pay attention to the main idea and important details.

Scanning for Information

After students have read the complete passage, they read the questions in this exercise, scan the complete passage for the answers, and either circle the correct answer or write the answer under each question. The last question in this section always refers to the main idea. When the students are finished, they may compare their answers with a classmate's. The pairs of students can then refer back to the passage and check their answers. The students may prefer to work in pairs throughout this exercise.

Word Forms

In order to successfully complete the *Word Forms* exercises in this book, the students will need to understand parts of speech, specifically nouns, verbs, adjectives, and adverbs. Teachers should point out the position of each word form in a sentence. Students will develop a sense for which part of speech is necessary in a given sentence. Because this is a low-level text, the *Word Forms* exercise simply asks students to identify the correct part of speech. They do not need to consider the tense of verbs or the number (singular or plural) of nouns.

To provide further vocabulary enrichment, a *Word Partnership* box highlights the common partners for one of the target words. These word partnerships, taken from *Heinle's Collins Cobuild School Dictionary of American English*, help students begin to notice which words often occur together.

Vocabulary in Context

This is a fill-in exercise designed as a review of the items in the previous exercises. The vocabulary has been highlighted either in the *Prereading Preparation* section or elsewhere in the chapter. This exercise may be done for homework as a review or in class as group work.

Topics for Discussion and Writing

This section provides ideas or questions for the students to think about and/or work on alone, in pairs, or in small groups. It provides beginning students with writing opportunities appropriate for their ability level, usually at the paragraph level. In addition, this section includes a *Write in your journal* question that encourages students to respond to a certain aspect of the reading.

Follow-up Activities

This section contains various activities appropriate to the information in the passages. Some activities are designed for pair and small group work. Students are encouraged to use the information and vocabulary from the passages both orally and in writing. The teacher may also use these questions and activities as home or in-class assignments. Some follow-up activities help the students interact with the real world by requiring them to go outside the classroom to interview people or to get specific information. In this way, students are not limited to speaking, reading, or learning in the classroom.

Crossword Puzzle

Each chapter contains a crossword puzzle based on the vocabulary used in that chapter. Crossword puzzles are especially effective when the students work in pairs. Working together provides students with an opportunity to speak together and to discuss their reasons for their answers.

If students need practice pronouncing the letters of the alphabet, they can go over the puzzle orally—the teacher can have the students spell out their answers in addition to pronouncing the words themselves. Students invariably enjoy doing crossword puzzles. They are a fun way to reinforce the vocabulary presented in the various exercises in each chapter, and they require students to pay attention to correct spelling.

Cloze Quiz

The *Cloze Quiz* is the reading passage itself with 10 to 20 vocabulary items omitted. The *Cloze Quiz* tests not only vocabulary but also sentence structure and comprehension in general. The students are given the words to be written in the blank spaces.

Index of Key Words and Phrases

At the back of the book is the *Index of Key Words and Phrases*. This section contains words and phrases from all the chapters for easy reference. This index can help students locate words they need or wish to review.

Acknowledgments

We are thankful to everyone at Heinle, especially Sherrise Roehr, Tom Jeffries, Laura Le Dréan, and Maryellen E. Killeen. As always, we are very appreciative of the ongoing encouragement from our family and friends.

L.C.S. and N.N.M.

Language and Culture

CHAPTER 1

Learning a Second Language

Prereading Preparation

1 Work with a partner. Make a list of things you can do to learn a second language. Complete the chart.

Things We Can Do to Learn a Second Language
1. Things frist idea about learn secound language.
2. speaking other peaple
3. writing withe teacher.
4. reading story and news peaper.
5. lestin. tv news.

2 Compare your list with your other classmates' lists. What can you add to your list?

_____

_____

_____

3 Read the title of this chapter. What will this passage discuss?

_____

Reading

Directions: Read each paragraph carefully. Then answer the questions.

Learning a Second Language

Some people learn a second language easily. Other people have trouble learning a new language. How can you help yourself learn a new language, such as English? There are several ways to make learning English a little easier and more interesting.

1 _____ True _____ False   Everyone learns a second language easily.

2 Other people have **trouble** learning a new language.
Trouble means

a. difficulty
b. classes
c. reasons

3 There are **several** ways to make learning English a little easier and more interesting.
Several means

a. easier
b. many
c. different

4 What do you think the next paragraph will discuss?

    a. Problems learning a new language

    b. Ways to learn a new language more easily

    c. Where to study a second language

    The first step is to feel positive about learning English. If you believe that you can learn, you will learn. Be patient. You do not have to understand everything all at once. It is natural to make mistakes when you learn something new. We can learn from our mistakes. In other words, do not worry about taking risks.

---

5 What does it mean to feel **positive** about learning English?

    a. If you believe you can learn, you will learn.

    b. You can understand everything all at once.

    c. You must make mistakes.

6 When you are **patient,** do you worry about learning English very quickly?

    a. Yes

    b. No

7 You do not have to understand everything **all at once.**

All at once means

    a. slowly

    b. easily

    c. right now

8 We can learn from our mistakes. **In other words,** do not worry about **taking risks.**

    a. What follows **in other words?**

        1. An opposite idea

        2. An example

        3. The same idea

    b. **Taking risks** means

        1. taking chances

        2. working hard

        3. feeling positive

9 What do you think the next paragraph will discuss?

   a. Different kinds of languages

   b. Making mistakes

   c. The second step

The second step is to practice your English. For example, write in a journal, or diary, every day. You will get used to writing in English, and you will feel comfortable expressing your ideas in English. After several weeks, you will see that your writing is improving. In addition, you must speak English every day. You can practice with your classmates outside class. You will all make mistakes, but gradually you will become comfortable communicating in English.

10 What is a **journal?**

   a. A diary

   b. Practice

   c. An example

11 How can you practice your English?

   a. Write in a journal every day

   b. Practice with your classmates after class

   c. Both **a** and **b**

12 **After several weeks** means

   a. after a few days

   b. when a few weeks are finished

   c. a week later

13 **In addition,** you must speak English every day.
What follows **in addition?**

   a. More information

   b. The same information

   c. The result

14 **Gradually** means

   a. quickly

   b. carefully

   c. slowly

15 You will all make mistakes, but gradually you will become comfortable **communicating** in English.

Communicating in English means

   a. speaking and listening
   b. reading
   c. studying

16 What will the next paragraph discuss?

   a. Making mistakes
   b. Feeling comfortable
   c. The third step

The third step is to keep a record of your language learning. You can write this in your journal. After each class, think about what you did. Did you answer a question correctly? Did you understand something the teacher explained? Perhaps the lesson was difficult, but you tried to understand it. Write these accomplishments in your journal.

17 When you **keep a record** of something,

   a. you write it on paper
   b. you remember it
   c. you tell someone

18 _____ True _____ False   You can keep a record of your language learning in your journal.

19 **Perhaps** means

   a. usually
   b. sometimes
   c. maybe

20 Write these **accomplishments** in your journal.

Accomplishments are

   a. successes
   b. mistakes
   c. lessons

You must be positive about learning English and believe that you can do it. It is important to practice every day and make a record of your <u>achievements</u>. You will enjoy learning English, and you will have more confidence in yourself.

21 **Achievements** are
   a. accomplishments
   b. lessons
   c. problems

22 Read the following actions. Which actions are accomplishments? Circle all answers.
   a. You asked a question in class.
   b. You brought a notebook and a pen to class.
   c. You made a mistake, but you understood why.
   d. You tried to answer a question.
   e. You spoke your native language to a classmate.

Directions: Read the complete passage. When you are finished, answer the questions that follow.

Track 01

Learning a Second Language

1   Some people learn a second language easily. Other people have trouble
2   learning a new language. How can you help yourself learn a new language, such
3   as English? There are several ways to make learning English a little easier and
4   more interesting.
5   The first step is to feel positive about learning English. If you believe that you
6   can learn, you will learn. Be patient. You do not have to understand everything
7   all at once. It is natural to make mistakes when you learn something new. We
8   can learn from our mistakes. In other words, do not worry about taking risks.
9   The second step is to practice your English. For example, write in a journal,
10 or diary, every day. You will get used to writing in English, and you will feel
11 comfortable expressing your ideas in English. After several weeks, you will see
12 that your writing is improving. In addition, you must speak English every day.

13	You can practice with your classmates outside class. You will all make mistakes,
14	but gradually you will become comfortable communicating in English.
15	The third step is to keep a record of your language learning. You can write
16	this in your journal. After each class, think about what you did. Did you answer
17	a question correctly? Did you understand something the teacher explained?
18	Perhaps the lesson was difficult, but you tried to understand it. Write these
19	accomplishments in your journal.
20	You must be positive about learning English and believe that you can do it.
21	It is important to practice every day and make a record of your achievements.
22	You will enjoy learning English, and you will have more confidence in yourself.

Scanning for Information

Read the questions. Then go back to the complete passage and scan quickly for the answers. Circle the letter of the correct answer, or write your answer in the space provided.

1 Are there ways to make learning a second language easier?
  a. Yes
  b. No

2 How many steps are there? _third_

3 Describe each step. Then give one <u>example of each step.</u>

a. _Feel positive. about learn English_

b. _Practice Reding English._
write pregraph.

c. _In addition, you maust speak English every day._

4 What is the <u>main idea</u> of this story?
a. It is very important to learn a second language.
b. Some people learn a second language easily. Other people do not.
c. There are ways to help you learn a second language more easily.

B

Word Forms

In English, some adjectives (adj.) become adverbs (adv.) by adding the suffix -*ly*, for example, *brief* (adj.), *briefly* (adv.). Read the following sentences. Decide if the correct word is an adjective or an adverb. Circle your answer. Do the example as a class before you begin.

<u>Example:</u>

a. John spoke very brief / briefly at the meeting.
               (adj.)   *(adv.)*

b. John gave a very brief / briefly speech because he had to leave early.
               (adj.)   *(adv.)*

1 This is an <u>easy / easily</u> exercise.
        (adj.)   *(adv.)*

2 I can write the answers <u>easy / easily.</u>
               (adj.)   *(adv.)*

3 What is the <u>correct / correctly</u> answer?
         (adj.)   *(adv.)*

4 The students answered the question <u>correct / correctly</u>.
                                                 (adj.)   *(adv.)*

5 Every day our English <u>gradual / gradually</u> improves.
                                    (adj.)   *(adv.)*

6 This <u>gradual / gradually</u> improvement is exciting.
              (adj.)   *(adv.)*

7 Many people can speak a second language very <u>natural / naturally</u>.
                                                                    (adj.)   *(adv.)*

8 Children are <u>natural / naturally</u> language learners.
                   (adj.)   *(adv.)*

Word Partnership	Use *natural* with
adv.	**perfectly** natural
n.	natural **beauty**, natural **disaster**, natural **food**, natural **reaction**, natural **tendency**

C Vocabulary in Context

Read the sentences. Choose the correct word or phrase for each sentence. Write your answers on the blank lines.

all at once	**patient** *(adj.)*	**risks** *(n.)*

1 Alice enjoys trying new, exciting activities. She really likes to take

_____ .

2 You can't learn to use a computer _____ . It takes time to

learn everything you need to know.

3 My mother is a very _____ person. She always takes her time and is never in a hurry to finish something.

gradual (adj.)	in other words	positive (adj.)

4 Clark played the violin every day for four months. He saw a _____ improvement in his music.

5 I will take a math test tomorrow. I have studied hard, so I feel very _____ about the test.

6 Lucy eats fresh fruit and vegetables every day. She exercises five times a week, and she sleeps eight hours a night. _____, Lucy has a very healthy life.

confidence (n.)	in addition	perhaps (adv.)	trouble (n.)

7 John is very tired today. _____perhaps_____ he didn't sleep well last night. I'll ask him.

8 We didn't take care of our car. Last week we went on vacation, and we had _____trouble_____ with our car.

9 Tony needs to have more _____confidence_____. He is always afraid of doing something wrong.

10 Peter went to the store. He bought milk, meat, bread, and fruit. _____in addition_____, he got coffee and tea.

D Topics for Discussion and Writing

1 Imagine that you have a friend who plans to come to the United States to study English. Write a letter to your friend. Tell your friend what to expect. Give your friend advice about learning English more easily.

2 When do you use English the most? Where? Write about this and give examples.

3 Where do you prefer to study (for example, at home, in the library, etc.)? Do you like to study alone or with a friend? Why? Talk about this with your classmates.

4 Start a journal of your language learning. Use a small notebook that will be easy to carry with you. Write in your journal several times a week. Do you think your English is improving? Why? Write about your language learning accomplishments.

Follow-up Activities

1. What is the most difficult part of learning English for you? Talk to several of your classmates. Ask them for suggestions to help you. Talk to several people outside your class. Ask them for suggestions, too. Try some of these suggestions and then report back to your classmates. Tell them which suggestions were the most helpful and explain why.

2. Refer back to your list of things you can do to learn a language. Work with a partner. Talk about your lists. Decide *where* you can do these activities, and *which language skills* each activity will help you develop. Write them in the chart below. There is an example to help you.

Activity	Skills (listening, speaking, reading, writing)	Where Can You Do This Activity?
I ask questions when I don't understand.	speaking and listening	in class, in stores, on the street, at a train station or a bus stop, on the telephone
news peaper, T.V uwriting and reding if idant understand i ask questions and study with friend	writing and reding speeking	oo home, in class in trivel, on coffe — make friend; movie

Crossword Puzzle

Read the clues on the next page. Write the answers in the correct spaces in the puzzle.

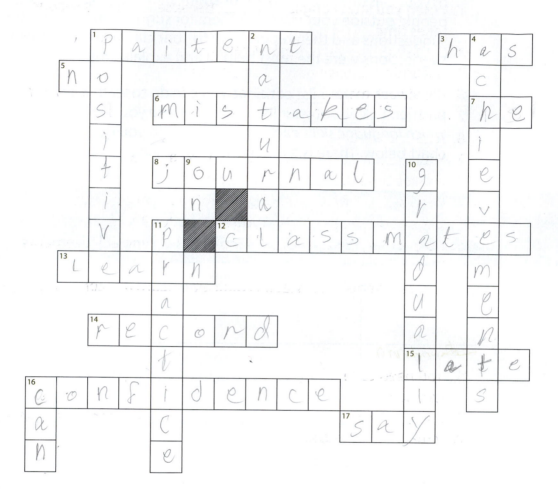

Crossword Puzzle Clues

1. When you study English, be _____ because learning a second language takes time.
3. English _has_ many irregular verbs.
5. Is learning English easy? _no_ , it isn't.
6. We always make _mistakes_, or errors, when we learn something new.
7. **She, _____ , it**
8. A _____ is a diary.
12. Your _____ are the other students in your class.
13. It takes time to _le_ a second language.
14. Keep a _____ of your language learning in your diary.
15. Class begins at 9 o'clock. If you arrive after 9, you are _late_.
16. Keep a diary and write your language learning achievements. This will give you _____ .
17. Most students _____ that it is difficult to learn a second language.

1. You need to feel very _____ about learning English. You need to say that you can do it!
2. It is _____ , or normal, to make errors when you learn a second language.
4. Your _____ , or accomplishments, will help you feel more comfortable.
9. Your pen is _____ your desk.
10. Slowly; after a long time.
11. It is important to _____ English every day.
16. You _can_ learn English!

G Cloze Quiz

Read the following passage. Fill in the blanks with the correct words from the list. Use each word only once.

easily	interesting	learn	such	trouble

Some people learn a second language _____(1). Other people have _____trouble_____(2) learning a new language. How can you help yourself _____(3) a new language, _____such_____(4) as English? There are several ways to make learning English a little easier and more _____interesting_____(5).

achievements	believe	confidence	positive	practice

You must be _____positive_____(6) about learning English, and you must _____(7) that you can do it. It is important to _____practice_____(8) every day and make a record of all your _____achievements_____(9). You will enjoy learning English, and you will have more _____confidence_____(10) in yourself.

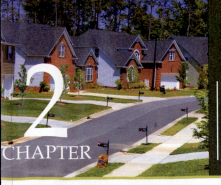

2 CHAPTER

The Best Place to Live

Prereading Preparation

1 Look at the photograph. What are the people doing?

   a. Cleaning a new house
   b. Moving into a new house
   c. Leaving a new house

2 Why is this family doing this? Write one reason here. Then talk about some reasons with your classmates.

ching my live.
buy new home.
learning other languege.

3 Work with a partner. Read the title of this chapter. Where do you think is the best place to live? Why do you think so? Complete the chart.

	The Best Place to Live	Reasons
You	go to Islands	small place littl people
Your Partner	home in china	home twon, with his family

Reading

Directions: Read each paragraph carefully. Then answer the questions.

The Best Place to Live

Do you like your hometown? Are you happy there? Most Americans like where they live. In fact, 80 percent of Americans say that they like their hometowns very much. They are happy there. A large number of Americans—almost 40 percent—live in the same place all their lives. They never live anywhere else. However, some other Americans are ready for a change.

1 _____ True _____ False   Your **hometown** is the place where you live.

2 _____ True _____ False   Most Americans are happy in their hometowns.

3 _____ True _____ False   Most Americans live in the same place all their lives.

4 **Some other Americans are ready for a change** means
   a. they want a new job
   b. they want a new place to live
   c. they want to change their clothes

urban /rural /suburbs

Forty-six percent of all Americans say they want to live in a different location. They like their hometowns, but they would like to move somewhere else. For example, some people who live in a city want to live in a small town. Some city dwellers want to move to a rural area, or countryside, because they don't like cities. Other people want to live in the suburbs, which are areas near cities. However, many people who live in small towns and rural areas are not happy either. They prefer to live in a different kind of place.

5 **Forty-six percent of all Americans** means

   a. most Americans
   b. all Americans
   c. some Americans

6 A **location** is

   a. a town
   b. a city
   c. a place

7 **Somewhere else** means

   a. a town
   b. a city
   c. another place

8 **City dwellers** are people who

   a. live in a city
   b. work in a city
   c. live at home

9 Other people want to live in the **suburbs,** which are areas near cities. The **suburbs** are

   a. in cities
   b. close to cities
   c. far from cities

10 **However, many people who live in small towns and rural areas are not happy either.**

Who isn't happy?

a. Some people who live in the city.
b. Some people who live in small towns.
c. Some people who live in the city and some people who live in small towns.

11 A **rural area** is in

a. a city
b. the countryside
c. a town

Of course, not everyone agrees on the best place to live. Different people choose to live in different places. For instance, young people prefer to live in cities. They choose big cities like New York, Boston, and Los Angeles. Martin Beck agrees with this. He lives in Boston. "I love living in the city," says Martin. "There are great museums, restaurants, and movie theaters. There are a lot of jobs here, too."

12 _____ True _____ False   All Americans agree on the best place to live.

13 Where do many young Americans like to live?

They choose big cities like New York, Boston.

14 _____ True _____ False   Martin Beck is a young person.

15 Where does Martin live?

a. In a small town
b. In a big city
c. In a museum

16 Does Martin like where he lives?

a. Yes
b. No
c. I don't know.

17 Why do some Americans like to live in big cities?

There are a lot of jobs here, museums, restaurants, and movies

4

On the other hand, many older Americans prefer to live in smaller towns. For example, Janet and Mario Miller and their family live in a small town in Idaho. Janet says, "I love our town! We know all of our neighbors. The schools here are small and the streets are always quiet." Yet the majority of Americans—young and old—agree on one idea: They prefer warm weather to cold weather.

Even though some people dream about moving somewhere else, most people are happy with their hometowns. Where do you want to live?

18 **On the other hand** shows
- **a.** a new idea
- **b.** an opposite idea
- **c.** something you are holding

19 Who prefers to live in smaller towns?
- **a.** All older Americans
- **b.** All Americans
- **c.** Some Americans

20 _____ True _____ False   Janet and Mario Miller are older Americans.

21 Where does the Miller family live?
- **a.** In a big city
- **b.** In a warm place
- **c.** In a small town

22 Janet says, **"I love our town! We know all of our neighbors…"**

Neighbors are people who
- **a.** work with you
- **b.** live near you
- **c.** go to school with you

23 Why does Janet like her small town?

beacouse she knew all of our neighbors.

24 Yet the **majority** of Americans—young and old—agree on one idea:
They prefer warm weather to cold weather.

Majority means

 a. some
 b. all
 c. most

25 Which sentence is correct?

 a. Most Americans like warm weather better than cold weather.
 b. Most Americans like cold weather better than warm weather.

26 **Even though some people dream about moving somewhere else, most
people are happy with their hometowns.**

This sentence means

 a. most people do not want to move to a different place
 b. most people want to move to a different place
 c. most people will be happy in a different place

Directions: Read the complete passage. When you are finished, answer the
questions that follow.

Track 02

The Best Place to Live

1   Do you like your hometown? Are you happy there? Most Americans
2 like where they live. In fact, 80 percent of Americans say that they like their
3 hometowns very much. They are happy there. A large number of Americans—
4 almost 40 percent—live in the same place all their lives. They never live
5 anywhere else. However, some other Americans are ready for a change.
6   Forty-six percent of all Americans say they want to live in a different location.
7 They like their hometowns, but they would like to move somewhere else. For
8 example, some people who live in a city want to live in a small town. Some
9 city dwellers want to move to a rural area, or countryside, because they don't
10 like cities. Other people want to live in the suburbs, which are areas near cities.
11 However, many people who live in small towns and rural areas are not happy
12 either. They prefer to live in a different kind of place.

UNIT 1   LANGUAGE AND CULTURE

13   Of course, not everyone agrees on the best place to live. Different people
14 choose to live in different places. For instance, young people prefer to live in
15 cities. They choose big cities like New York, Boston, and Los Angeles. Martin
16 Beck agrees with this. He lives in Boston. "I love living in the city," says Martin.
17 "There are great museums, restaurants, and movie theaters. There are a lot of
18 jobs here, too."

19   On the other hand, many older Americans prefer to live in smaller towns. For
20 example, Janet and Mario Miller and their family live in a small town in Idaho.
21 Janet says, "I love our town! We know all of our neighbors. The schools here are
22 small and the streets are always quiet." Yet the majority of Americans—young
23 and old—agree on one idea: They prefer warm weather to cold weather.

24   Even though some people dream about moving somewhere else, most people
25 are happy with their hometowns. Where do you want to live?

Homes in the Suburbs

Scanning for Information

Read the questions. Then go back to the complete passage and scan quickly for the answers. Circle the letter of the correct answer, or write your answer in the space provided.

1 Complete each sentence with the correct number.

　　a. _46_ percent of Americans want to live in a different place.

　　b. _40_ percent of Americans never move to a different place.

　　c. _80_ percent of Americans like their hometowns a lot.

2 **a.** Where do some young people prefer to live?

　　　 in the big city

　　b. What are reasons for this?

　　　1. _museums._

　　　2. _restaurants._

　　　3. _movie_

3 **a.** Where do some older people prefer to live?

　　　 small town.

　　b. What are reasons for this?

　　　1. _They are know the neighbers._

　　　2. _The stree are aluns quite._

　　　3. _____

4 What is the main idea of this story?

　　a. A large number of Americans live in the same place all their lives.

　　b. Many older Americans prefer to live in the city.

　　c. Most Americans are happy where they live, but some are ready for a change.

B Word Forms

choese name

A

An

The

In English, some adjectives (adj.) become nouns (n.) by adding the suffix *–ness*, for example, *kind* (adj), *kindness* (n.). Read the following sentences. Decide if the correct word is an adjective or a noun. Circle your answer. Do the example below as a class before you begin.

Example:

    a. Bob is a (shy) / shyness person. He is quiet and does not talk to his
           (adj.)   (n.)

    classmates very often.

    b. Bob's shy / (shyness) is the reason he has very few friends.
           (adj.)   (n.)

1 Annie lives in a very (small) / smallness apartment.
              (adj.)   (n.)

2 Only 3,000 people live in my hometown. I know everyone there because of the small / (smallness) of the town.
           (adj.)   (n.)

3 My family really enjoys the quiet / (quietness) of living in a rural area.
               (adj.)   (n.)

4 There are very few cars, trucks, or people! The countryside is really a very (quiet) / quietness place to live.
   (adj.)   (n.)

5 My grandmother always wears a sweater and a heavy jacket because of the *clothese* (cold) / coldness of the winter.
   (adj.)   (n.)

6 She often stays indoors on very (cold) / coldness days. She really prefers
                (adj.)   (n.)
   the summer!

7 Everyone talks about my sister's ready / (readiness) to help other people.
             (adj.)   (n.)

8 My sister is always (ready) / readiness to help others. She is a wonderful person.
         (adj.)   (n.)

9 Arthur and Jane are getting married next week. They are very
<u>happy / happiness</u>.
  (adj.)   *(n.)*

10 Their family and friends share their <u>happy / happiness</u>, too.
                                      (adj.)   *(n.)*

Word Partnership	Use *happy* with
adv.	**extremely/perfectly/very** happy
v.	**feel** happy, **make** *someone* happy, **seem** happy
n.	happy **ending**, happy **family**, happy **marriage**

I like to stay in my hometown

C Vocabulary in Context

Read the following sentences. Choose the correct word or phrase for each sentence. Write your answers on the blank lines.

anywhere else	**hometown** *(n.)*	**on the other hand**

1 Steven loves his _____. He never wants to move to another city.

2 Leigh feels lonely living away from her parents. _____, she enjoys her independence.

3 Tom usually buys shoes in this store. He can't find what he wants _____.

agrees (v.)	change (n.)	majority (n.)	neighbors (n.)

4 Marta thinks Italian food is delicious, and Tony _____ with her.

5 The _____ of Americans drink coffee with their breakfast.

6 My _____ always help me when I have a problem.

7 Tara will go to a new school next year. It will be a big _____ for her.

dweller (n.)	even though	rural (adj.)

8 In many _____ areas, the roads have no lights.

9 We love living in the countryside _____ we have to drive 15 miles to get to the nearest town.

10 Kim loves living in New York. She will always be a city _____.

D Topics for Discussion and Writing

1 Work with a partner. What are some reasons that people choose different places to live? Make a list with your partner. Discuss some of your reasons with your class.

2 What is most important to you when you choose a place to live? Why is this important? Explain your answer.

3 Do you think it is difficult or easy to move to a new place? Why? Write your answer and talk about it with your classmates.

4 **Write in your journal.** Do you like your city? Why or why not? Give reasons for your answer.

A Rural Home

Urban Homes

Follow-up Activities

1 Look at the charts below and answer the questions.

Where Do Americans Live Now?

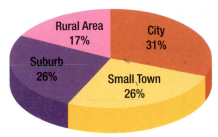

Source: Pew Research Center, U.S. survey, 2009

**Do Americans Think Their Hometown
Is the Best Place to Live?**

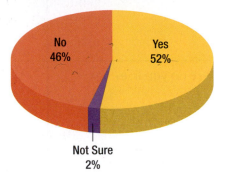

Source: Pew Research Center, U.S. survey, 2009

a. Where does the largest percentage of Americans live? ___in city___

b. Where does the smallest percentage of Americans live? ___Rural Area___

c. What <u>percentage</u> of Americans live in or near a city?
1. 26%
2. 52%
3. 57%

d. Are the majority of Americans happy where they live?
1. Yes
2. No

2 Ask your classmates the following questions and write their answers in the chart.

Survey of the Best Place to Live			
Name of Student	bill	Ibrahim	Ahmad
Where do you live?	kamloops	kamloops.	kamloops
Are you happy there?	yes	yes	yes
Why or why not?	kamloops is cbiet.	quiet and small	bencaus its beautiful
Do you want to live in another place?	yes, vancouver	No	No
Why or why not?	He bencous lik big city	.like kmlaps	like kamloops
Where do you want to live?	Frinsh.	.kamloops	kamloops

3 Compare your chart with your classmates' charts. Then discuss these questions with your class.

    a. Are most of your classmates happy where they live? Why or why not?

    b. Where do most students want to live? Why?

Crossword Puzzle

Read the clues on the next page. Write the answers in the correct spaces in the puzzle.

Across answers filled in: got, change, have, countryside, ready, take, different, all, somewhere, neighbor, very, else, yes

Crossword Puzzle Clues

3. The past tense of **get**
4. Nick needs to _____ his job. He hates his work.
7. I _____ ; **he has**
10. Rural areas are called the _____ .
12. John studied for three weeks. He is _____ for the test!
13. Please _____ this chair to another room.
14. These books are not the same. They are _____ .
15. Each; every
16. I don't like living here. I want to live _____ else.
18. My _____ lives in the house next to mine.
20. Mary passed the test. She is _____ happy.
21. I love the country! I don't want to live anywhere _____ .
22. The opposite of **no**

1. Your _____ is the place where you live.
2. Do you _____ milk or cream with your tea?
5. A _____ of people prefer to live in a warm place.
6. **One, two, three, _____**
8. The past tense of **is**
9. I would like to see you tomorrow. _____ , I have to stay home and study.
11. City _____ are people who live in cities.
15. If I _____ with you, I think the same as you.
17. _____ areas are far from the city.
19. The opposite of **sad**

G

Cloze Quiz

Read the following passages. Fill in the blanks with the correct words from the list. Use each word only once.

anywhere	change	happy	hometowns	place

Do you like your hometown? Are you _____ *happy* _____ (1) there? Most Americans like where they live. In fact, 80 percent of Americans say that they like their _____ *hom....* _____ (2) very much. They are happy there. A large number of Americans—almost 40 percent—live in the same _____ *place* _____ (3) all their lives. They never live _____ *anywhere* _____ (4) else. However, some other Americans are ready for a _____ *change* _____ (5).

countryside	dwellers	location	move	town

Forty-six percent of all Americans say they want to live in a different _____ *location* _____ (6). They like their hometowns, but they would like to _____ *move* _____ (7) somewhere else. For example, some people who live in a city want to live in a small _____ *town* _____ (8). Some city _____ *dwellers* _____ (9) want to move to a rural area, or the _____ *countryside* _____ (10), because they don't like cities. Other people want to live in the suburbs, which are areas near cities. However, many people who live in small towns and rural areas are not happy either. They prefer to live in a different kind of place.

Home and Family

The McCaugheys: An Unusual Family

Prereading Preparation

1 Look at the photograph. Work with a partner and answer the questions in the chart.

How many children are there?	How old are they?	Are they brothers and sisters?
Number _7_	_8_ months/years old	Yes _✓_ No _____

2 Read the title of this story. Why is this family unusual?

  a. They have young children.
  b. They have many young children.
  c. They have seven children the same age.

Reading

Directions: Read each paragraph carefully. Then answer the questions.

The McCaugheys: An Unusual Family

Kenny and Bobbi McCaughey live in Iowa. They have a big family. In fact, they have eight children. But this family is also very unusual. Mikayla is the oldest child in the family. She is six years old. The other children are Brandon, Joel, Kelsey, Kenny, Natalie, Alexis, and Nathan. They are all five years old. Why are they all the same age? Because they are septuplets! Septuplets are seven children who are born together.

1 Who are Kenny and Bobbi McCaughey?
   a. The parents
   b. The children

2 How many children do the McCaugheys have?
   a. Eight
   b. Seven
   c. Five

3 What are **septuplets?**
   a. Large families
   b. Seven children born together
   c. Five-year-old children

4 _____ True __✓__ False   Mikayla is a septuplet.

5 How old are the septuplets? __5 years old.__

It is hard work to take care of seven babies at the same time. But Kenny and Bobbi did not take care of the seven babies alone. In the beginning, many people helped them. The babies did not sleep a lot, so every day, eight or nine people came to the McCaughey house to help them. Their friends and families helped to feed, clean, and dress the babies. Every week, the septuplets used about 170 diapers! They drank a lot of milk, too.

6 _____ True _____ False   Many people helped Kenny and Bobbi.

7 _____ True _____ False   The septuplets slept a lot in the beginning.

8 Friends and families helped because septuplets
    a. are hard work
    b. drink a lot of milk
    c. are unusual

9 Their friends and families helped to feed, clean, and **dress** the babies.
Dress means
    a. to put a dress on the babies
    b. to put clothes on the babies

10 Babies use **diapers** because they
    a. can't drink from a cup
    b. can't use the bathroom

Now the children are older. Bobbi says, "It's easier to take care of the children now. They feed and dress themselves, and they don't need diapers anymore!" The septuplets started school this year. But they do not leave the house. Why? The children go to school at home, like their big sister, Mikayla. When Mikayla was ready for school, Kenny and Bobbi decided to teach her at home. "Homeschooling" is popular. Many families in the United States teach their children at home. The children do all their schoolwork at home. Last year, Bobbi was Mikayla's teacher. Now, Bobbi is the teacher for all eight of her children.

11 It's easier to take care of the septuplets now because
   a. they are older
   b. they go to school
   c. their big sister helps

12 _____ True ___✓___ False   The septuplets wear diapers now.

13 The septuplets are unusual students because they
   a. are not ready to go to school
   b. can't dress themselves
   c. go to school at home

14 Homeschooling is **popular.**
   Popular means
   a. many people like homeschooling
   b. homeschooling is very expensive
   c. homeschooling is easy to do

15 Who is the septuplets' teacher? ___Bobbi___

16 **Homeschooling** means that
   a. children do not learn
   b. children do not have teachers
   c. children learn at home

Directions: Read the complete passage. When you are finished, answer the questions that follow.

The McCaugheys: An Unusual Family

1 Kenny and Bobbi McCaughey live in Iowa. They have a big family. In fact,
2 they have eight children. But this family is also very unusual. Mikayla is the
3 oldest child in the family. She is six years old. The other children are Brandon,
4 Joel, Kelsey, Kenny, Natalie, Alexis, and Nathan. They are all five years old. Why
5 are they all the same age? Because they are septuplets! Septuplets are seven
6 children who are born together.

7 It is hard work to take care of seven babies at the same time. But Kenny and
8 Bobbi did not take care of the seven babies alone. In the beginning, many people
9 helped them. The babies did not sleep a lot, so every day, eight or nine people
10 came to the McCaughey house to help them. Their friends and families helped
11 to feed, clean, and dress the babies. Every week, the septuplets used about
12 170 diapers! They drank a lot of milk, too.

13 Now the children are older. Bobbi says, "It's easier to take care of the children
14 now. They feed and dress themselves, and they don't need diapers anymore!"
15 The septuplets started school this year. But they do not leave the house.
16 Why? The children go to school at home, like their big sister, Mikayla. When
17 Mikayla was ready for school, Kenny and Bobbi decided to teach her at home.
18 "Homeschooling" is popular. Many families in the United States teach their
19 children at home. The children do all their schoolwork at home. Last year,
20 Bobbi was Mikayla's teacher. Now, Bobbi is the teacher for all eight of her
21 children.

A Scanning for Information

Read the questions. Then go back to the complete passage and scan quickly for the answers. Circle the letter of the correct answer, or write your answer in the space provided.

1 Where does the McCaughey family live?

The one live in lowa.

2 Who helped Kenny and Bobbi McCaughey take care of the septuplets?

many people helped them. eight or nine friends.

3 Why don't the septuplets wear diapers anymore?

because new the children are older.

4 Why don't the children go to school?

the parents teache him at home.

5 What is the main idea of this story?

    a. It is hard work for parents to take care of septuplets.
    b. Homeschooling is very popular today in the United States.
    c. The McCaugheys are unusual because they have septuplets.

B Word Forms

In English, some words can be either a noun (n.) or a verb (v.), for example, *change*. Read the sentences below. Decide if the correct word is a noun or a verb. Circle your answer. Do the example below as a class before you begin.

Example:

    a. We change / change our clothes every day.
            (v.)   (n.)

    b. The change / change in the weather made me sick.
            (v.)   (n.)

1 Kenny and Bobbi did not get very much <u>sleep / sleep</u> at first.
   (v.) (n.)

2 The septuplets did not <u>sleep / sleep</u> very much at first.
   (v.) (n.)

3 The family <u>uses / uses</u> a room in their house as a classroom.
   (v.) (n.)

4 One room has many <u>uses / uses</u>. It is a classroom, a playroom,
   and a living room.   (v.) (n.)

5 Do you always <u>work / work</u> during the day?
   (v.) (n.)

6 I do my <u>work / work</u> for school at night.
   (v.) (n.)

7 The septuplets got a good <u>start / start</u> in life because so many people
   helped them.   (v.) (n.)

8 I sometimes <u>start / start</u> my day by reading the newspaper.
   (v.) (n.)

9 Kenny's and Bobbi's families <u>help / help</u> them with the children.
   (v.) (n.)

10 Kenny and Bobbi don't need a lot of <u>help / help</u> now because the
   children are older.   (v.) (n.)

Word Partnership	Use *help* with
adj.	**financial** help, **professional** help
v.	**ask for** help, **get** help, **need** help, **try to** help, **want to** help, **cry/scream/shout for** help, **can't** help **thinking/feeling** *something*

Vocabulary in Context

Read the following sentences. Choose the correct word for each sentence.
Write your answers on the blank lines. *7 children born same time* *Journal.*

hard *(adj.)*	helped *(v.)*	septuplets *(n.)*	together *(adv.)*
3	4	1	2

1 _____ are seven children who are born at the same time.

2 Brandon, Joel, Kelsey, Kenny, Natalie, Alexis, and Nathan are all five years

old. They were born _____ .

3 It is difficult to take care of seven babies. It is _____ work.

4 Many people _____ the McCaugheys. They cleaned and

dressed the children.

feed *(v.)*	ready *(adj.)*	*not comp* unusual *(adv.)*
5	7	6

5 Every day, eight or nine people came to _____ the babies.

6 The McCaughey family is _____ because they have

septuplets.

7 Most children are _____ for school when they are five

years old.

decided (v.)	popular (adj.)	teacher (n.)

8 Bobbi is the _____ for all her children.

9 Homeschooling is _____ in the United States. Many people do it.

10 Bobbi and Kenny _____ to homeschool the children. The children do not leave the house for school.

D Topics for Discussion and Writing

1 Bobbi is homeschooling her children. What subjects does she teach? Work in pairs and write a schedule for the McCaugheys' school day.

_____

_____

_____

_____

_____

2 What will happen when the children are older? Will they go to school when they are teenagers? Or will Bobbi continue to homeschool them? What do you think? Share your ideas with your classmates.

3 Why do some people decide to homeschool their children? Think about possible reasons and discuss them with your classmates.

4 **Write in your journal.** Do you think homeschooling is a good idea? Why or why not? Write a paragraph to explain your opinion.

Follow-up Activities

E

1 Work in a small group. The McCaugheys' septuplets are five years old now. How much food do you think they eat in one day? Complete the chart.

	Breakfast	Lunch	Dinner
Drinks	1 gallon of orange juice		
Food			
Dessert			
Snacks			

2 Work in a group. Write a list of questions you want to ask the septuplets. Then exchange your list with another group. Try to answer the other group's questions.

Questions	Answers
1.	1.
2.	2.
3.	3.
4.	4.
5.	5.

Crossword Puzzle

Read the clues on the next page. Write the answers in the correct spaces in the puzzle.

Crossword Puzzle Clues

3. The McCaugheys got _____ from their families and friends.
6. Only _____ child is not a septuplet.
8. The seven children were born at the _____ time.
10. _____ are seven children who are born at the same time.
11. Did Kenny and Bobbi _____ to teach the children at home? Yes!
13. When the septuplets were babies, they used 170 _____ every week.
14. Mikayla is _____ one of the septuplets.
16. The McCaughey family lives in _Iowa_ . It is a state in the United States.
17. Bobbi is homeschooling her children. _she_ is their teacher.
18. The children do not _go_ to school. They study at home.
20. Mikayla is _older_ than the septuplets.

1. _all_ of the children learn at home.
2. The septuplets can _dress_ themselves now. They can put on their clothes by themselves.
3. _homeschooling_ is very popular in the United States and in other countries, too.
4. The seven younger children were born _____ . They were born on the same day.
5. Teaching children at home is very _____ . Many parents do it.
7. Septuplets are _____ children who are born at the same time.
9. Family and friends helped to _____ the children breakfast, lunch, and dinner.
12. Having eight children _____ a lot of work!
15. The McCaugheys are a very _____ family.
19. Feeding, dressing, and caring for eight children is _hard_ work.

Cloze Quiz

Read the passage below. Fill in the blanks with the correct words from the list.
Use each word only once.

alone	feed	hard	help	milk

It is _____hard_____ (1) work to take care of seven babies at the

same time. But Kenny and Bobbi did not take care of the seven babies

_____alone_____ (2) . In the beginning, many people helped them. The babies

did not sleep a lot, so every day, eight or nine people came to the McCaughey

house to _____help_____ (3) them. Their friends and families helped to

_____feed_____ (4) , clean, and dress the babies. Every week, the septuplets

used about 170 diapers! They drank a lot of _____milk_____ (5) , too.

easier	leave	older	popular	ready

Now the children are _____older_____ (6) . Bobbi says, "It's

_____easier_____ (7) to take care of the children now. They feed and dress

themselves, and they don't need diapers anymore!" The septuplets started

school this year. But they do not _____ready_____ (8) the house. Why? The

children go to school at home, like their big sister, Mikayla. When Mikayla

was _____leave_____ (9) for school, Kenny and Bobbi decided to teach her at

home. "Homeschooling" is _____popular_____ (10) . Many families in the United

States teach their children at home. Now, Bobbi is the teacher for all eight of

her children.

A Musical Family

Prereading Preparation

Look at the photo. Read the title of the story. Then answer the questions in the chart.

Questions	Answers
1. What are these people holding?	
2. How many children are in the picture?	
3. What musical instruments do you see?	

Reading

Directions: Read each paragraph carefully. Then answer the questions.

A Musical Family

Shawn and Whitney Cabey-Gray lived with their _four_ children in the city of Chicago. Every night, the family ate dinner together. Most of the time, the children talked about video games. The oldest child, Nick, did not like to talk about school. He was not doing well in math. Shawn and Whitney were very unhappy. They did not want this life for their children. Four years ago, they decided to make a change. What did they do?

1 Where did this family live? _chicago_

2 Who are Shawn and Whitney?
   a. The parents
   b. The children

3 _____ True __✓__ False   The family played video games together every night.

4 __✓__ True _____ False   The family ate dinner together every night.

5 What did the children talk about at dinner?
   video games

6 Did Nick like to talk about school? _No_

7 **Nick was not doing well in math** means
   a. he did not like math
   b. he did not get good grades in math
   c. he did good work in math

8 Why were Shawn and Whitney unhappy?
   a. They did not like to eat dinner together.
   b. They did not like to talk about video games.
   c. They did not like this life for the family.

9 They **decided** to make a change.

Decide means

   a. make a choice
   b. talk about
   c. fight about

10 Answer this question: **What did they do?**

_____

> Shawn and Whitney sold their house in Chicago. They threw away the video games and moved a thousand miles away to a very small town in Maine. Whitney decided to homeschool the children. Nick began to enjoy math. His schoolwork improved, and the other children's did, too.

11 Where did the family go? _the went to main_

12 _____ True __✓__ False   Maine is near Chicago.

13 Who is the children's teacher? _shawn and whitney_

14 Why did Whitney decide to homeschool the children?

   a. She wanted to help them do better.
   b. She didn't like their teacher.
   c. The school was 1,000 miles away.

15 Nick began to **enjoy** math.

Enjoy means

   a. do
   b. work
   c. like

16 His schoolwork **improved**, and the other children's did, too.

Improve means

   a. become harder
   b. become better
   c. become enjoyable

17 __✓__ True _____ False   The children's schoolwork improved.

All the children enjoyed their new lives, but sometimes they were bored. Shawn decided to give them music lessons. Now every afternoon, they play their music together. Each child plays a different musical instrument. Nick is 16 years old. He plays the viola. Zack, who is 13 years old, plays the cello. Twelve-year-old Bryanna, the only daughter in the family, plays the violin. The youngest child in the family is Noah. He is only six years old, but he plays the piano very well. In fact, he plays it better than his father! The children love to perform together, and Shawn and Whitney love to listen to them.

Now the Cabey-Gray family has a very different life. The town is quiet, but the Cabey-Gray's house is not!

18 All the children enjoyed their new lives, but sometimes they were **bored. Bored** means

    a. they had a lot of schoolwork to do
    b. they did not have a lot of interesting things to do
    c. they did not have a lot of friends

19 Why did Shawn give them music lessons?

    a. The parents love to listen to the children.
    b. The children didn't enjoy their new lives.
    c. The children were bored.

20 Who is the oldest child? _____16 years_____

21 Who is the youngest child? _____Noah_____

22 How many daughters do Shawn and Whitney have?
_____one doter_____

23 **The children love to perform together** means

    a. the children love to play music together
    b. the children love to study together
    c. the children love to live in Maine together

24 Why isn't the Cabey-Gray's house quiet?
_____play music_____

Directions: Read the complete passage. When you are finished, answer the questions that follow.

A Musical Family

1   Shawn and Whitney Cabey-Gray lived with their four children in the city
2   of Chicago. Every night, the family ate dinner together. Most of the time, the
3   children talked about video games. The oldest child, Nick, did not like to talk
4   about school. He was not doing well in math. Shawn and Whitney were very
5   unhappy. They did not want this life for their children. Four years ago, they
6   decided to make a change. What did they do?
7   Shawn and Whitney sold their house in Chicago. They threw away the
8   video games and moved a thousand miles away to a very small town in Maine.
9   Whitney decided to homeschool the children. Nick began to enjoy math. His
10 schoolwork improved, and the other children's did, too.
11   All the children enjoyed their new lives, but sometimes they were bored.
12 Shawn decided to give them music lessons. Now every afternoon, they play
13 their music together. Each child plays a different musical instrument. Nick is
14 16 years old. He plays the viola. Zack, who is 13 years old, plays the cello.
15 Twelve-year-old Bryanna, the only daughter in the family, plays the violin. The
16 youngest child in the family is Noah. He is only six years old, but he plays the
17 piano very well. In fact, he plays it better than his father! The children love to
18 perform together, and Shawn and Whitney love to listen to them.
19   Now the Cabey-Gray family has a very different life. The town is quiet, but
20 the Cabey-Gray's house is not!

Scanning for Information

Read the following questions. Then go back to the complete passage and scan quickly for the answers. Circle the letter of the correct answer, or write your answer in the space provided.

1 Why did the Cabey-Gray family move from Chicago to Maine?

Becose are they happy

2 What changes did the Cabey-Gray family make?

a. _The did not want this liet for ther children._

b. _Four years ago they decided to make a chang._

c. _besaid homeschool._

3 All the children enjoyed their new lives, but sometimes they were **bored.** Shawn decided to give them music lessons.

Why were the children bored?

because they dent have any activity

4 How is the Cabey-Gray family's life different now?

a. _the town is quiet_

b. _Each childre like play music._

5 What is the main idea of this story?

a. The Cabey-Gray children love to perform music together.

b. The Cabey-Gray parents wanted their family to have a better life.

c. The Cabey-Gray children's schoolwork improved a lot in Maine.

Word Forms

In English, some words can be either a noun (n.) or a verb (v.), for example, *work*. Read the sentences below. Decide if the correct word is a noun or a verb. Circle your answer. Do the example as a class before you begin.

Example:

a. I have a lot of work / work to do today.
                 (v.)   (n.)

b. When I am busy, I work / work 10 or 11 hours in a day!
                    (v.)   (n.)

1 The Lee family will move / move to Florida next month.
                   (v.)   (n.)

2 They are very happy about the move / move.
                     (v.)   (n.)

3 Shawn and Whitney love / love the children very much.
                  (v.) (n.)

4 The children have a good life because of their parents' love / love.
                              (v.) (n.)

5 The Cabey-Gray family decided to change / change their life.
                   (v.)   (n.)

6 The change / change was very important to the family.
   (v.)   (n.)

Word Partnership	Use **change** with
v.	**adapt to** change, **make a** change
adj.	**gradual** change, **sudden** change
n.	change of **address**, change **clothes**, change **color**, change **direction**

Vocabulary in Context

Read the following sentences. Choose the correct word or phrase for each sentence. Write your answers on the blank lines.

| bored *(adj.)* | enjoyed *(v.)* | quiet *(adj.)* |

1. The small town in Maine is a very ___*quiet*___ place to live.

2. The children became ___*bored*___ because they did not have a lot to do.

3. After they moved, the children _____ their new lives in Maine.

| improve *(v.)* | perform *(v.)* | unhappy *(adj.)* |

4. Shawn and Whitney were ___*unhappy*___ in Chicago. They did not like their lives.

5. The children play their musical instruments. They ___*perform*___ together in their home.

6. Whitney homeschooled the children, and Nick's schoolwork started to ___*improve*___ .

| decided *(v.)* | lessons *(n.)* | plays *(v.)* | threw away *(v.)* |

7. Noah ___*plays*___ the piano very well.

8. Bryanna ___*decided*___ to play the violin, but Zack wanted to play the cello.

9 The parents ___*threw away*___ the children's video games. They did not want the children to play them anymore.

10 Shawn taught the children to play musical instruments. He gave music ___*lessons*___ to them.

Topics for Discussion and Writing

1 The Cabey-Gray family moved from a large city to a small town. Do you want to live in a large city or a small town? Explain your answer.

2 Can you play a musical instrument? Write about it. Or write about a musical instrument you want to play. Why do you want to play this instrument?

3 The Cabey-Gray family enjoys playing music together. What do you like to do with your family? Is it important to do this together? Why? Write a paragraph and give examples.

4 **Write in your journal.** Do you think the Cabey-Gray family has a better life now? Why or why not?

Follow-Up Activities

1 In this chapter, the parents made a decision and changed their family's life. They moved 1,000 miles away from a big city to a small town. This is a very big change. Work in a group. Imagine you are Shawn or Whitney. You are unhappy, but you *don't* want to move far away. What other ways can you change your lives? Complete the chart.

	Changes in . . .
our children's lives	
our lives	
our family's life	

2 The Cabey-Gray family moved to a different town. What changes did Shawn and Whitney make in their lives? Work with a partner and complete the chart.

Changes in Whitney's Life	Changes in Shawn's Life
1.	1.
2.	2.
3.	3.

Crossword Puzzle

Read the clues on the next page. Write the answers in the correct spaces in the puzzle.

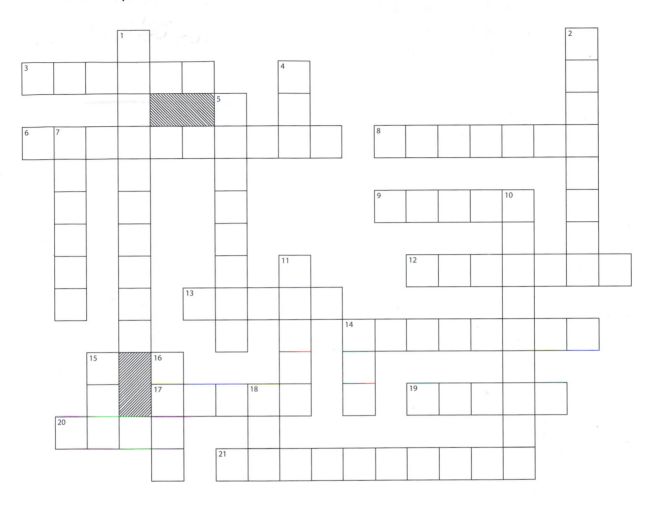

Crossword Puzzle Clues

ACROSS CLUES

3. When I make a choice, I _____ .
6. Shawn and Whitney Cabey-Gray _____ their children. They do not send their children to school to learn.
8. When we become better at something, we _____ .
9. We feel _____ when we do not have something interesting to do.
12. The children sometimes _____ with their father – they are a five-person band.
13. Nick began to _____ math when his mother taught him. She made it fun!
14. Noah is the _____ child in the family. All the other children are older.
17. Each; all
19. The Cabey-Gray family _____ from a city to a small town.
20. A _____ has 365 days.
21. A violin is a musical _____ .

DOWN CLUES

1. In Chicago, the children played _____ (two words), but they don't play them anymore.
2. The children perform _____ . They are a band.
4. In the Cabey-Gray family, _____ people play the piano: Noah and his father.
5. Maine is a _____ miles from Chicago. They are very far from each other.
7. Nick is the _____ child. All the other children are younger.
10. Each child plays something _____ . Nick plays the viola, Zack plays the cello, Bryanna plays the violin, and Noah plays the piano.
11. The opposite of **quiet**
14. The opposite of **no**
15. Noah plays _____ piano.
16. The Cabey-Gray family is _____ happy now.
18. Walk very fast

Cloze Quiz

Read the passage below. Fill in the blanks with the correct words from the list.
Use each word only once.

began	enjoyed	improved	moved	sold

Shawn and Whitney _____sold_____ their house in Chicago. They
threw away the video games and _____moved_____ 1,000 miles away to a
(2)
very small town in Maine. Whitney decided to homeschool the children. Nick
_____improved_____ to enjoy math. His schoolwork _____began_____ , and
(3)   (4)
the other children's did, too. All the children _____enjoyed_____ their new
(5)
lives, but sometimes they were bored.

decided	different	only	together	youngest

Shawn _____decided_____ to give them music lessons. Now, every
(6)
afternoon they play their music _____together_____ . Each child plays a
(7)
_____different_____ musical instrument. Nick is 16 years old. He plays the
(8)
viola. Zack, who is 13 years old, plays the cello. Twelve-year-old Bryanna,
the _____only_____ daughter in the family, plays the violin. The
(9)
_____youngest_____ child in the family is Noah. He is only six years old,
(10)
but he plays the piano very well.

UNIT 3

Exercise and Fitness

5
CHAPTER

The Importance of Exercise for Children

Prereading Preparation

1 Look at the photograph. What are the children doing?

a. Playing soccer
b. Playing roller hockey
c. Ice skating

2 Work with a partner from another country. Discuss the questions in the information chart and fill in the answers.

What country are you from?	Do children exercise in school?	How often do children exercise in school?	What kinds of exercise do the children do?
1. china	yes	twice week	soccer
2.	yes		snow bonding

3 Read the title of this story. What do you think the reading will discuss?

Reading

Directions: Read each paragraph carefully. Then answer the questions.

The Importance of Exercise for Children

Joseph is a very busy eight-year-old boy. In the fall, he plays on a roller hockey team. He practices every Tuesday and Thursday afternoon and has a roller hockey game every Sunday morning. In the winter, Joseph plays basketball. His team practices one evening a week. They have a basketball game every Saturday morning. In the spring and summer, Joseph plays baseball. His team has a game twice a week and practices at least once. It is easy to see that Joseph is very active after school.

1 Why is Joseph **a very busy eight-year-old boy?**

    a. He goes to school a lot.
    b. He plays many different sports.
    c. He plays on a roller hockey team.

2 His team practices **one evening a week.**

    One evening a week means

    a. every night during the week
    b. at 1:00 during the week
    c. one night every week

    activity action

3 It's easy to see that Joseph is very active **after** school.

    Why is **after** underlined?

    a. For emphasis
    b. Because it is a new word
    c. To show a contrast

4 What do you think the next paragraph will discuss?

_____

In contrast, while most American children are in school, they have a physical education class just once a week for 45 minutes. Boys and girls from kindergarten to grade 12 do not have to have a physical education class in school every day. They do not have to exercise.

Not all American children are as active in sports after school as Joseph is. Therefore, these boys and girls need to exercise in school. Many people believe that the fitness and health of American children are in trouble. In fact, 40% of children aged five to eight may be unhealthy already. For example, many have high blood pressure, are overweight, or have high cholesterol. Doctors believe that these conditions are the result of physical inactivity and poor diet.

5 **In contrast,** while most American children are in school, they have a **physical education class** just once a week for 45 minutes.

In contrast shows

  a. an example
  b. a similarity
  c. a difference

6 What is a **physical education class?**

  a. A science class
  b. An exercise class
  c. An outdoor class

7 How often do most American children exercise in school?

one a week for 45 minutes

8 _____ True __✓__ False   Most school children have a physical education class every day in the United States.

9 **Not all American children are as active in sports after school as Joseph is. Therefore,** these boys and girls need to exercise in school.

  a. The first sentence means that many American children

    1. are also very active in sports, like Joseph
    2. are more active in sports than Joseph is
    3. are less active in sports than Joseph is

  b. **Therefore** means

    1. also
    2. as a result
    3. for example

10 Many people believe that the **fitness** and health of American children are **in trouble.**

   a. (Fitness) means

      1. good physical condition
      ②. exercise
      3. sports

   b. Many people believe that the fitness and health of American children

      1. are in America
      2. are interesting
      ③. are a problem

11 ____✓___ True _____ False   Many American children may be unhealthy already.

12 Doctors believe that these conditions are the result of **physical inactivity** and poor diet.

   What is **physical inactivity?**

   a. Sports
   b. No exercise
   c. High blood pressure

> In many countries in the world, all schoolchildren have to do one hour of exercise every day. These exercises do not have to be team sports. They may be simple, such as running, jumping, or climbing ropes. Doctors believe that habits learned early are more likely to stay with us through life. School is the perfect place to learn these habits, or practices. Active, healthy children who exercise regularly = *often* can become active, healthy adults.

13 _____ True __✓__ False   Running, jumping, and climbing rope are always team sports.

14 Doctors believe that **habits** learned early are more likely to **stay with us through life.** School is the perfect place to learn **these habits,** or practices.

   a. **Habits** are

      1. places
      2. sports
      ③. practices

b. What are **these habits?**

1. Reading habits
2. Exercise habits
3. Study habits

c. **Stay with us through life** means

1. we will continue to do it
2. we will start these habits early
3. we will not change

15 _____/_____ True _____ False   The author believes that American children need to exercise in school more often.

Directions: Read the complete passage. When you are finished, answer the questions that follow.

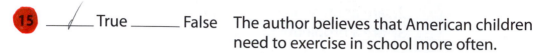

Track 05

The Importance of Exercise for Children

1 Joseph is a very busy eight-year-old boy. In the fall, he plays on a roller
2 hockey team. He practices every Tuesday and Thursday afternoon and has
3 a roller hockey game every Sunday morning. In the winter, Joseph plays
4 basketball. His team practices one evening a week. They have a basketball game
5 every Saturday morning. In the spring and summer, Joseph plays baseball. His
6 team has a game twice a week and practices at least once. It is easy to see that
7 Joseph is very active <u>after</u> school.
8   In contrast, while most American children are <u>in</u> school, they have a
9 physical education class just once a week for 45 minutes. Boys and girls from
10 kindergarten to grade 12 do not have to have a physical education class in school
11 every day. They do not have to exercise.
12   Not all American children are as active in sports after school as Joseph is.
13 Therefore, these boys and girls need to exercise in school. Many people believe
14 that the <u>fitness</u> and health of American children are in trouble. In fact, 40% of
15 children aged five to eight may be unhealthy already. For example, many have
16 high blood pressure, are overweight, or have high cholesterol. Doctors believe
17 that these conditions are the result of physical inactivity and poor diet.

18
19
20
21
22
23

In many countries in the world, all schoolchildren have to do one hour of exercise every day. These exercises do not have to be team sports. They may be simple, such as running, jumping, or climbing ropes. Doctors believe that habits learned early are more likely to stay with us through life. School is the perfect place to learn these habits, or practices. Active, healthy children who exercise regularly can become active, healthy adults.

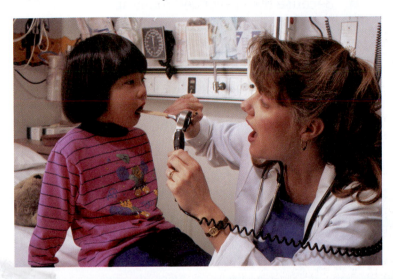

A

Scanning for Information

Read the questions. Then go back to the complete passage and scan quickly for the answers. Circle the letter of the correct answer, or write your answer in the space provided.

1 What sports does Joseph play after school?

Hocey, ponscthal, basketball

2 How often do most American children exercise <u>in</u> school?

once a week for

CHAPTER 5   THE IMPORTANCE OF EXERCISE FOR CHILDREN

3 **a.** Is physical activity important for children? _____yes_____

b. What can happen when children do not exercise?

they will be lazy, unhealthy, High blood

4 Active, healthy children who exercise regularly can become active, healthy adults. Why?

a. Because they were healthy children
b. Because they practiced many sports
c. Because they will continue their healthy habits

5 What is the main idea of this story?

a. Joseph does not exercise in school.
b. It is very important for children to exercise in school.
c. Schoolchildren around the world exercise every day.

B

Word Forms

In English, some words can be either nouns (n.) or verbs (v.), for example, *drink*. Read the following sentences. Decide if the word is a noun or a verb. Circle your answer. Do the example below as a class before you begin.

Example:

a. I always drink / drink water when I exercise.
         (n.)   (v.)

b. This drink / drink is very cold.
      (n.)   (v.)

1 Liz practices / practices the piano for one hour every day.
      (n.)   (v.)

2 Piano practice / practice is fun for her.
      (n.)   (v.)

3 Exercise / Exercise is important to our health.
     (n.)   (v.)

4 We exercise / exercise every afternoon.
      (n.)   (v.)

5 Tom made many <u>changes</u> / <u>changes</u> in his lifestyle.
     (n.)   (v.)

6 Tom also <u>changed</u> / <u>changed</u> his eating habits.
     (n.)   (v.)

7 I sometimes <u>diet</u> / <u>diet</u> to lose weight.
     (n.)   (v.)

8 My <u>diet</u> / <u>diet</u> includes a lot of fruit and vegetables.
     (n.)   (v.)

Word Partnership	Use *diet* with
adj.	**balanced** diet, **healthy** diet, **proper** diet, **strict** diet
n.	diet **and exercise**, diet **supplements,** diet **pills**
prep.	**on a** diet

Vocabulary in Context

Read the following sentences. Choose the correct word or phrase for each sentence. Write your answers on the blank lines.

at least	**habit** (n.)	**in contrast**

minimum

1 It is a good _____ to exercise three times a week. I usually exercise on Mondays, Thursdays, and Saturdays.

2 Eric doesn't enjoy team sports. _____, his brother Kyle plays basketball, baseball, and roller hockey.

3 I try to eat _____ two pieces of fruit every day. I always eat an apple and a banana. Sometimes I eat an orange, too.

active *(adj.)*	as a result	practice *(v.)*	regularly *(adv.)*

(handwritten: peggy 6 · 5 Conclusion · 7 · 4 often)

4 Many adults exercise _____. For example, some people run every morning before work.

5 Many children don't exercise every day. _____, some children are overweight.

6 Joseph is a very _____ child. He exercises all the time and plays many kinds of sports.

7 If you want to be a good swimmer, you must _____. You must swim several times a week.

condition *(n.)*	likely *(adj.)*	therefore

(handwritten: 8 · 10 · 9)

8 Some children are overweight. This _____ is sometimes a result of a poor diet.

9 Lynn's doctor told her to lose weight. _____, she is trying to eat less and exercise more.

10 Children who exercise are _____ to grow up and continue to exercise as adults.

D Topics for Discussion and Writing

1. Write a weekly exercise plan for yourself. Write a letter to your friend and describe your new plan.

2. When you were a child, did you exercise in school? How often did you exercise? What kind of exercise did you do? Discuss this with your classmates.

3. What is your favorite kind of exercise? For example, do you like to play a sport or take a walk? Write about your favorite kind of exercise. Why do you enjoy it? Explain your answer.

4. **Write in your journal.** Describe the most exciting sports event you have ever watched or participated in. What was the event? What happened? Why was it exciting for you?

E Follow-up Activities

1   Refer to all the physical activities you and your classmates listed at the beginning of this chapter. Put these activities into the appropriate categories of **Sports, Exercise,** and **Martial Arts** in the chart below. Some activities may belong in more than one category. For example, *swimming* can be a sport or an exercise.

Sports	Exercise	Martial Arts
swimming	swimming	

2   Imagine that a friend has asked you to give suggestions for activities that children can do in order to get exercise. Work with two or three classmates. Make a list of ten ways that children can get exercise that would be fun for them. When you are finished, write your suggestions on the blackboard. As a class, decide which ten activities children will enjoy the most.

_____

_____

_____

_____

_____

Crossword Puzzle

Read the clues on the next page. Write the answers in the correct spaces in the puzzle.

Crossword Puzzle Clues

1. Joseph _____ roller hockey games on Sunday mornings.
2. Joseph is physically active, _____ many children are not.
3. Soccer, basketball, and baseball are _____ .
5. Soccer and baseball _____ outdoor sports.
7. Children _____ exercise to be healthy.
8. Some children have a poor _____ . This means that they do not eat healthy food.
10. Exercise can be _____ . It can be enjoyable.
12. When children sit too much, they do not get enough _____ activity.
15. Joseph needs to exercise all his _____ , not just while he is a child.
17. A team needs to _____ every week.
18. Joseph is a very _____ boy. He plays on many teams after school.
19. Some children are very _____ with sports. They play after school and on weekends, too.

1. Regular exercise and a healthy diet are good _____ that we need all our lives.
3. **He, _____ , it**
4. A person who is heavy, or fat, is _____ .
6. Everyone needs to exercise _____ . We need to exercise every week.
9. Children can do all kinds of _____ , for example, running, jumping, or climbing rope.
11. Some conditions, such as being overweight, can be _____ .
13. Joseph exercises every day. In _____ , some children do not exercise at all.
14. Physical _____ means being in good physical condition.
16. We can do some sports alone, for example, running. We do other sports with a _____ .

G

Cloze Quiz

Read the following paragraphs. Fill in each space with the correct word from the list. Use each word only once.

busy	every	practices	winter
easy	morning	week	

Joseph is a very _____ eight-year-old boy. In the fall,
(1)

he plays on a roller hockey team. He _____ every Tuesday
(2)

and Thursday afternoon and has a roller hockey game every Sunday

_____ . In the _____ , Joseph plays basketball.
(3)   (4)

His team has a basketball game _____ Saturday morning. In
(5)

the spring and summer, Joseph plays baseball. His team has a game twice a

_____ and practices often. It is _____ to see that
(6)   (7)

Joseph is very active <u>after</u> school.

active	exercise	result	trouble
believe	overweight	therefore	unhealthy

Not all American children are as _____ in sports after
(8)

school as Joseph is. _____ , these boys and girls need to
(9)

_____ in school. Many people believe that the fitness and
(10)

health of American children are in _____ . In fact, 40% of
(11)

children aged five to eight may be _____ already. For example,
(12)

many have high blood pressure, are _____ , or have high
(13)

cholesterol. Doctors _____ that these conditions are the
(14)

_____ of physical inactivity and poor diet.
(15)

6
CHAPTER

The New York City Marathon[1]: A World Race

Prereading Preparation

1 Look at the photo. How many people do you think are running in this marathon?

2 Read the title of this chapter. Why is the New York City Marathon a world race? Where is this race? Who runs in this race?

3 Work with two or three classmates. What are some reasons why people run in marathons? Make a list. Compare your list with your classmates' lists.

[1] **marathon:** a foot race about 26 miles (about 43 kilometers) long

Reading

Directions: Read each paragraph carefully. Then answer the questions.

The New York City Marathon: A World Race

The New York City Marathon was started by a man named Fred Lebow. It began in 1970 as a small, unimportant race. Only 127 people ran, and just 55 of them finished. They ran around Central Park four times. Few people watched them run. However, over the years, the marathon grew and became more popular.

Today, people come from all over the world to run in the marathon. Runners must be at least 18 years old, but there is no age limit. In fact, the oldest runner was an 89-year-old man. Recently, more than 43,000 people ran in the New York City Marathon. Large crowds cheered the runners and offered the participants cold drinks and encouragement.

1 Only 127 people ran, and **just** 55 of them finished.

Just means

a. because
b. only
c. more than

2 _____ True _____ False   All 127 people finished the first marathon.

3 However, **over the years**, the marathon grew and became more popular.

Over the years means

a. as the years went by
b. one year after
c. many more years

4 _____ True _____ False   Runners cannot be younger than 18 years old.

5 **There is no age limit** means

a. people of any age can run
b. older people cannot run
c. anyone older than 18 years old can run

The course of the marathon has changed, too. Instead of running around Central Park, the participants go through the five boroughs of New York City: Queens, Brooklyn, Manhattan, the Bronx, and Staten Island. The marathon begins at the base of the Verrazano Narrows Bridge in Staten Island. The runners go across the bridge into Brooklyn. Then they go up through Queens and into the Bronx. The marathon finishes in Central Park in Manhattan. The complete course is 26 miles, 385 yards, and takes the best runners less than three hours.

6 The **course** of the marathon has changed, too.

In this sentence, **course** means

a. direction
b. class
c. reason

7 Instead of running around Central Park, the **participants** go through the five boroughs of New York City…

The **participants** are

a. the crowd
b. the runners
c. the organizers

8 _____ True _____ False   The fastest runners can finish the race in three hours or more.

Although it has changed since 1970, the New York City Marathon is always exciting. Through the years, many unusual events have happened during the marathon. For example, Pat Tuz and John Weilbaker got married a few minutes before the race. Then they ran the race with their wedding party. Some people run the whole marathon as a family. Other people run the race backwards. In the fall of 1992, Fred Lebow, the founder of the New York City Marathon, slowly ran his last race. He was very ill with cancer, but he did not want to stop running. In October 1994, Fred died. However, the New York City Marathon, and all its excitement, will continue for many years to come.

9 _____ True _____ False   Pat Tuz and John Weilbaker ran the marathon backwards.

UNIT 3   EXERCISE AND FITNESS

10 _____ True ___✓___ False   Fred Lebow ran his last race in 1994.

11 **In the fall** of 1992, Fred Lebow, the founder of the New York City Marathon, slowly ran his last race.

In the fall means

a. when someone fell down
b. the time before winter
c. the beginning of the year

New York City Marathon Route
(total distance 26.2 miles)

Track 06

The New York City Marathon: A World Race

1 The New York City Marathon was started by a man named Fred Lebow. It
2 began in 1970 as a small, unimportant race. Only 127 people ran, and just 55
3 of them finished. They ran around Central Park four times. Few people
4 watched them run. However, over the years, the marathon grew and became
5 more popular.

6 Today, people come from all over the world to run in the marathon. Runners
7 must be at least 18 years old, but there is no age limit. In fact, the oldest runner
8 was an 89-year-old man. Recently, more than 43,000 people ran in the New York
9 City Marathon. Large crowds cheered the runners and offered the participants
10 cold drinks and encouragement.

11 The course of the marathon has changed, too. Instead of running around
12 Central Park, the participants go through the five boroughs of New York City:
13 Queens, Brooklyn, Manhattan, the Bronx, and Staten Island. The marathon
14 begins at the base of the Verrazano Narrows Bridge in Staten Island. The
15 runners go across the bridge into Brooklyn. Then they go up through Queens
16 and into the Bronx. The marathon finishes in Central Park in Manhattan.
17 The complete course is 26 miles, 385 yards, and takes the best runners less
18 than three hours.

19 Although it has changed since 1970, the New York City Marathon is
20 always exciting. Through the years, many unusual events have happened
21 during the marathon. For example, Pat Tuz and John Weilbaker got married a
22 few minutes before the race. Then they ran the race with their wedding party.
23 Some people run the whole marathon as a family. Other people run the race
24 backwards.

25 In the fall of 1992, Fred Lebow, the founder of the New York City Marathon,
26 slowly ran his last race. He was very ill with cancer, but he did not want to stop
27 running. In October 1994, Fred died. However, the New York City Marathon,
28 and all its excitement, will continue for many years to come.

Scanning for Information

Read the questions. Then go back to the complete passage and scan quickly for the answers. Circle the letter of the correct answer, or write your answer in the space provided.

1 Describe two ways that the New York City Marathon has changed.

a. _more popular_

b. _____

2 What do the crowds do during the marathon?

cheer

3 What are some unusual events that have happened during the marathon?

other people ran backward

4 What is the main idea of this story?

a. The New York City Marathon began in 1970.

b. The founder of the New York City Marathon was an important man.

c. The New York City Marathon is a very popular and exciting race.

Word Forms

In English, some verbs (v.) can become nouns (n.) by adding the suffix *-ment,* for example, *agree* (v.), *agreement* (n.). Read the following sentences. Decide if the correct word is a noun or a verb. Circle your answer. Do the example as a class before you begin.

Example:

a. My wife and I agree / agreement that we will live in a big city.
   (v.)   (n.)

b. This agree / agreement is very important to us.
   (v.)   (n.)

1. The crowds excite / excitement the runners in the marathon.
   (v.)   (n.)

2. There is a lot of excite / excitement all day.
   (v.)   (n.)

3. Many people encourage / encouragement the runners by cheering.
   (v.)   (n.)

4. The crowd's encourage / encouragement is very important to the runners.
   (v.)   (n.)

5. English is a require / requirement in all American universities.
   (v.)   (n.)

6. American universities also require / requirement a high school degree.
   (v.)   (n.)

7. Andy has made a lot of improve / improvement in his English this semester.
   (v.)   (n.)

8. Every day Andy's English improves / improvement a little more.
   (v.)   (n.)

Word Partnership	Use *improve* with
v.	**continue to** improve, **expected to** improve, **try to** improve
adv.	**significantly** improve, improve **slightly**

Vocabulary in Context

Read the following sentences. Choose the correct word for each sentence. Write your answers on the blank lines.

cheer *(v.)*	encouragement *(n.)*	instead of

1. The crowds _____ *cheer* _____ when they watch baseball games.

2. I want to go swimming, but it is raining. _____ *instead of* _____ going to the beach, I will go to the indoor swimming pool at the college.

3. My parents always believed I could succeed. Their _____ *encouragement* _____ helped me to do well in school.

course *(n.)*	just *(adv.)*	limit *(n.)*	popular *(adj.)*

4. Marathons are very _____ *popular* _____ in American cities.

5. The speed _____ *limit* _____ on this highway is 55 miles an hour. You cannot drive faster than 55.

6. Olivia runs two miles every day. She follows a _____ *course* _____ through the park near her home.

7. I am taking _____ *just* _____ one class this semester because I have a job. I don't have time to take more than one class.

| however | participant *(n.)* | unusual *(adj.)* |

8 Snow is _____unusual_____ in New York City in April. It very rarely happens.

9 Robert wants to be a _____participant_____ in the next New York City Marathon. He runs 25 miles every week to prepare himself.

10 It is usually very cold in January. _____however_____, this year it was mild.

D Topics for Discussion and Writing

1 Work with two or three classmates. Have you or your partners ever run in a marathon? How did you prepare for it? What was the race like? If you haven't run in a marathon, do you want to? Why or why not?

2 Imagine that your friend wants to run in a marathon. In your group, discuss some advice that you can give your friend. Compare your suggestions with your other classmates' suggestions. Which suggestions are the best? Write a letter to your friend and give him or her your advice.

3 What is your favorite activity to participate in? In your group, discuss what you each like to do the most, for example, play soccer, run, play tennis, cycle, swim.

4 **Write in your journal.** Describe a popular sports event in your country. What is the event? Who participates? Why do people enjoy watching it?

Follow-up Activities

E

1 The following chart shows the number of participants in the New York City Marathon from 1970 through 2009. Look at it carefully and then read the statements. Circle *Yes* or *No*.

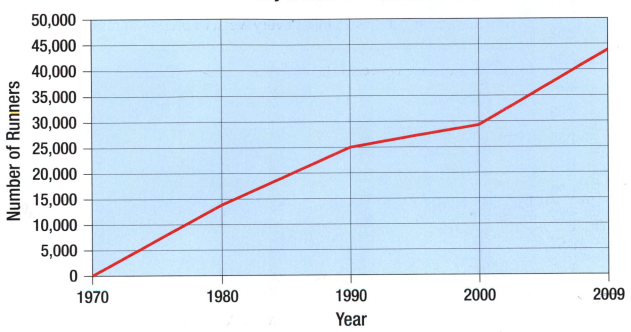

New York City Marathon – Number of Runners

a. More than 15,000 people ran in the New York City Marathon in 1980.
   1. Yes   2. No

b. About 25,000 people ran in the New York City Marathon in 1990.
   1. Yes   2. No

c. Almost 30,000 people ran in the New York City Marathon in 2000.
   1. Yes   2. No

d. More than 43,000 people ran in the New York City Marathon in 2009.
   1. Yes   2. No

e. The smallest increase in the number of runners occurred from 1990 to 2000.
   1. Yes   2. No

2 The following chart shows the finishing times of the men and women participants in the New York City Marathon from 1970 through 2009. Look at it carefully. Then read the sentences that follow. Complete each sentence with the word *women* or *men* to make it correct.

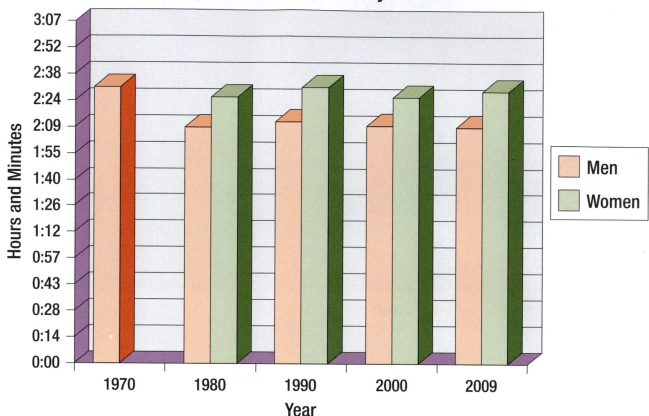

Winning Times for New York City Marathon

a. In 1970, only ___man___ ran in the Marathon.

b. In 1980, the winning time for ___man___ was 2 hours, 9 minutes.

c. In 1990, the winning time for ___women___ was 2 hours, 30 minutes.

d. In 2009, the winning time for ___women___ was 2 hours, 9 minutes.

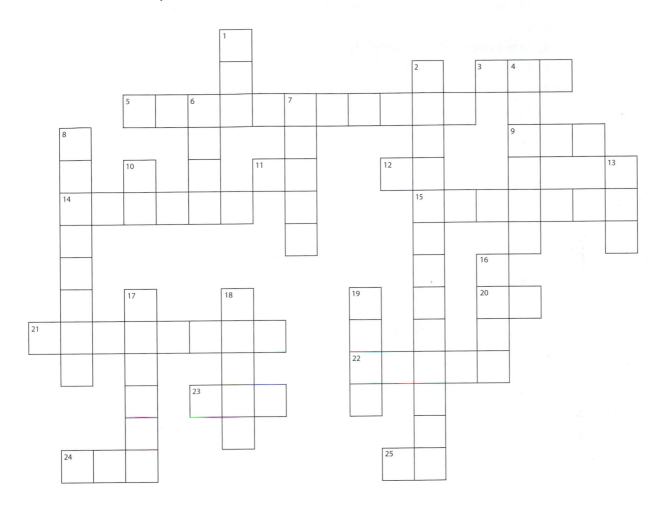

Crossword Puzzle

Read the clues on the next page. Write the answers in the correct spaces in the puzzle.

Crossword Puzzle Clues

3. Thousands of people begin the race, but not everyone _____ finish it.
5. Each _____ in the race gets a number for identification.
9. Most people _____ in the race, but some people simply walk fast.
11. Many people want _____ run in the New York City race.
12. People from all over the world _____ to New York City to be in the race.
14. Every _____ has trained for many months.
15. Sometimes people do _____, or strange, things during the race.
20. **I, me; we, _____**
21. Brooklyn, Queens, Manhattan, Staten Island, and the Bronx are the five _____ of New York City.
22. There is no age _____ for the race. Some very old people have run in this race.
23. At the end of the race, all the athletes _____ a medal.
24. **He, _____, it**
25. The race begins _____ the base of the Verrazano Narrows Bridge in Staten Island.

1. Only a few people win the race, _____ everyone feels successful.
2. The people who watch the race offer _____ to the runners.
4. Everyone runs _____ the bridge from Staten Island to Brooklyn.
6. The _____ is about 26 miles in length.
7. A huge _____ of people lines the route of the race in order to watch.
8. A _____ is a 26-mile race.
10. The race is always held _____ a Sunday.
13. Each; every
16. In the first race, _____ half the people finished.
17. The _____ of the race runs through all the boroughs of New York City.
18. The people who watch the race _____ as the runners pass them on the route.
19. The race is always held in the _____, when the weather is cool.

Cloze Quiz

Read the following paragraphs. Fill in the blanks with the correct words from the list. Use each word only once.

cheered	limit	oldest	recently
encouragement	marathon	participants	

Today, people come from all over the world to run in the ___marathon___ (1). Runners must be at least 18 yeas old, but there is no age ___limit___ (2). In fact, the ___oldest___ (3) runner was an 89-year-old man. ___recently___ (4), more than 43,000 people ran in the New York City Marathon. Large crowds ___cheered___ (5) the runners and offered the ___participants___ (6) cold drinks and ___encouragement___ (7).

backwards	example	race	since
events	exciting	ran	whole

Although it has changed ___since___ (8) 1970, the New York City Marathon is always ___exciting___ (9). Through the years, many unusual ___event___ (10) have happened during the marathon. For ___example___ (11), Pat Tuz and John Weilbaker got married a few minutes before the ___race___ (12). Then they ___ran___ (13) the race with their wedding party. Some people run the ___whole___ (14) marathon as a family. Other people run the race ___backwards___ (15).

Remarkable Researchers

UNIT

4

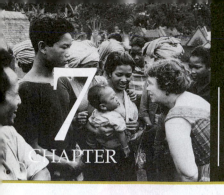

7 CHAPTER

Margaret Mead: The World Was Her Home

Prereading Preparation

Work with a classmate to discuss these questions.

1. Look at the photograph. The woman on the right was Margaret Mead. She was American.

    a. What was her occupation? What do you think?

    1. She was an artist.
    2. She was an anthropologist.
    3. She was a doctor.

    b. What kind of work did Margaret Mead do?

    1. She helped sick people.
    2. She painted pictures.
    3. She studied different cultures.

    c. Where did Margaret Mead do most of her work?

    1. In her own country
    2. In a hospital
    3. In different countries

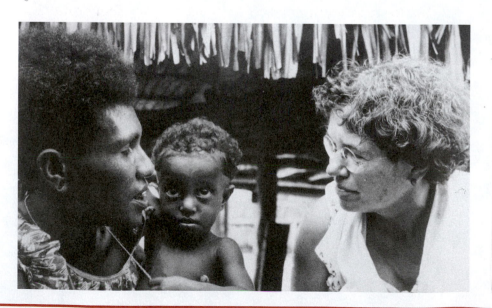

2 Describe the kind of work that you think Margaret Mead did. Write one or two sentences.

_____

_____

3 Read the title of this chapter. Why do you think the whole world was Margaret Mead's home? How can the world be a person's home?

_____

_____

Reading

Directions: Read each paragraph carefully. Then answer the questions.

Margaret Mead: The World Was Her Home

Margaret Mead was a famous American anthropologist. She was born on December 16, 1901, in Philadelphia, Pennsylvania. She lived with her parents, her grandmother, and her brother and sisters. Her parents were both teachers, and her grandmother was a teacher, too. They believed that education was very important for children. They also believed that the world was important. Margaret learned many things from her parents and grandmother.

When she was a child, Margaret's family traveled often and lived in many different towns. Margaret was always interested in people and places, so she decided to study anthropology in college to learn about different cultures. At that time it was not very common for women to study in a university. It was even more unusual for women to study anthropology.

1 _____ True __✓__ False   Margaret Mead's parents were anthropologists.

2 What do these two paragraphs discuss?
   a. Margaret's education as a young child
   b. The importance of Margaret's family and childhood
   c. The importance of Margaret's occupation

3 Why did Margaret decide to study anthropology?

she decide to study anthropology?

4 What do you think the next part of the story will discuss?

It was even more unusual for women to study anthropology.

Margaret graduated from college in 1923. She wanted to continue her education in anthropology, so she decided to go to American Samoa to study about young women there. Many people did not know about the culture of American Samoa. Margaret wanted to learn about Samoans so that the world could learn about them, too.

Margaret lived in Samoa for nine months and learned the language. She talked with the Samoan people, especially the teenage girls. She ate with them, danced with them, and learned many details about their peaceful culture.

5 ____✓____ True _____ False   Margaret went to Samoa to continue her education in anthropology.

6 Why did Margaret want to learn about the Samoan culture?
- **a.** She wanted to go to college in Samoa.
- **b.** She wanted to teach the world about Samoa.
- **c.** She wanted to learn the Samoan language.

7 How long did Margaret live in Samoa? ___9 month___

8 _____ True ____✓____ False   Margaret knew the Samoan language before she went to Samoa.

9 She talked with the Samoan people, **especially** the **teenage girls.**
- **a. Especially** means
  1. only
  2. most importantly
  3. except for
- **b. Teenage girls** are
  1. girls from 13 to 19 years old
  2. girls from 7 to 14 years old
  3. girls over 18 years old

10 _____ True _____ False   The Samoan culture was peaceful.

When Margaret returned to the United States, she wrote a book about the young Samoan women she studied. The book was called *Coming of Age in Samoa*, and it was very popular. As a result, Margaret Mead became very famous. Before Margaret wrote her book, not many people were interested in anthropology. Because of Margaret's book, anthropology became a popular subject.

Margaret Mead studied many different cultures in her life. She continued to work, travel, write, and teach until she died in 1978. She was a remarkable woman of the world.

11 *Coming of Age in Samoa* was

   a. a book
   b. a magazine
   c. a teenage girl

12 What was the subject of Margaret's book?

13 Why did Margaret Mead become famous?

   a. Because she was an anthropologist
   b. Because she studied many cultures
   c. Because she wrote a popular book

14 Margaret Mead continued to work, travel, write, and teach **until** she died in 1978.

   a. **Until** means
      1. when something begins
      2. when something continues
      3. when something stops

   b. Complete the sentence: Last night Elizabeth studied at the library **until**
      1. it opened
      2. it closed
      3. she woke up

15 Margaret Mead was a **remarkable** woman of the world. **Remarkable** means

    a. educated

    b. hardworking

    c. unusual

Directions: Read the complete passage. When you are finished, answer the questions that follow.

Track 07

Margaret Mead: The World Was Her Home

1   Margaret Mead was a famous American anthropologist. She was born
2 on December 16, 1901, in Philadelphia, Pennsylvania. She lived with her
3 parents, her grandmother, and her brother and sisters. Her parents were
4 both teachers, and her grandmother was a teacher, too. They believed that
5 education was very important for children. They also believed that the
6 world was important. Margaret learned many things from her parents
7 and grandmother.

8   When she was a child, Margaret's family traveled often and lived in many
9 different towns. Margaret was always interested in people and places, so she
10 decided to study anthropology in college to learn about different cultures. At
11 that time it was not very common for women to study in a university. It was
12 even more unusual for women to study anthropology.

13   Margaret graduated from college in 1923. She wanted to continue her
14 education in anthropology, so she decided to go to American Samoa to study
15 about young women there. Many people did not know about the culture of
16 American Samoa. Margaret wanted to learn about Samoans so that the world
17 could learn about them, too.

18   Margaret lived in Samoa for nine months and learned the language.
19 She talked with the Samoan people, especially the teenage girls. She ate
20 with them, danced with them, and learned many details about their
21 peaceful culture.

22   When Margaret returned to the United States, she wrote a book about the
23 young Samoan women she studied. The book was called *Coming of Age in Samoa*,
24 and it was very popular. As a result, Margaret Mead became very famous. Before
25 Margaret wrote her book, not many people were interested in anthropology.
26 Because of Margaret's book, anthropology became a popular subject.

27   Margaret Mead studied many different cultures in her life. She continued
28 to work, travel, write, and teach until she died in 1978. She was a remarkable
29 woman of the world.

A Scanning for Information

Read the questions. Then go back to the complete passage and scan quickly for
the answers. Circle the letter of the correct answer, or write your answer.

1 Margaret Mead decided to study anthropology in college to learn about
different cultures.

a. Why do you think she made this decision?

_____

b. Was this an unusual decision? Why or why not?

_____

2 How did Margaret study the Samoan people?

_____

3 What did Margaret Mead contribute to anthropology? In other words, why was Margaret Mead important to anthropology?

_____

_____

4 What is the main idea of this story?
   a. Margaret Mead was interested in different cultures.
   b. Margaret Mead wrote a book about Samoan women.
   c. Margaret Mead helped to make anthropology a popular subject.

B

Word Forms

In English, some verbs (v.) become nouns (n.) by adding the suffix -ence or -ance to the verb. Read the following sentences. Decide if the correct word is a noun or a verb. Circle your answer.

1 Children depend / dependence on their parents for everything.
      (v.)   (n.)

2 This depend / dependence usually continues until they complete
      (v.)   (n.)
high school.

3 Eric's appears / appearance is changing in many ways as be becomes older.
      (v.)   (n.)

4 For example, he appears / appearance thinner, and his hair is turning gray.
      (v.)   (n.)

5 Sharks prefer warm water. They avoid / avoidance cold water.
      (v.)   (n.)

6 Their avoid / avoidance of cold water helps them to survive.
      (v.)   (n.)

7 My sister and I differ / difference from each other in many ways.
   (v.)   (n.)

8 Because of our differ / differences, we are not very close.
   (v.)   (n.)

Word Partnership	Use *difference* with
adj.	**big/major** difference
v.	**know the** difference, **notice a** difference, **tell the** difference, **settle a** difference, **pay the** difference, **make a** difference
n.	difference **in age**, difference **in price**

C Vocabulary in Context

Read the following sentences. Choose the correct word or phrase for each sentence. Write your answers on the blank lines.

believe (v.)	**especially** (adv.)	**remarkable** (adj.)

1 Helen enjoys all her classes, but she _____ likes her English class. That is her favorite subject.

2 Sharks are _____ animals. They hunt for food at night by feeling vibrations in the water.

3 My brother and I exercise every day. We _____ that exercise is important for good health.

as a result	**cultures** (n.)	**peaceful** (adj.)

4 The Samoans are very _____ people. They rarely disagree or fight with each other.

5 Choi and Marina come from different _____ , but they are very good friends.

6 Maria did not do her homework last night. _____ , she was not prepared for class today.

details *(n.)*	interested *(adj.)*	popular *(adj.)*	until *(prep.)*

7 That is a very _____ type of car. Many people buy it because it is inexpensive and reliable.

8 Cesar is _____ in medicine. He wants to become a doctor.

9 I studied last night _____ midnight. Then I went to sleep.

10 There was an earthquake in California this morning, but I don't know the _____ . I want to listen to the radio to learn more about it.

D   Topics for Discussion and Writing

1 Write a paragraph. Describe one or two interesting things you have learned about American culture. How did you learn these things about American culture?

2 Describe someone important in your culture. This may be someone who is alive now or who lived in the past. Write a paragraph about this person. When you are finished, exchange papers with a classmate and read each other's descriptions. Then discuss what you learned about your classmate's culture by reading about this person.

3 Do you think anthropology is important? Why or why not? Write a paragraph to explain your opinion. Give examples.

4 **Write in your journal.** Imagine that you are a student of anthropology. Decide what culture you want to study. Discuss your reasons in a paragraph.

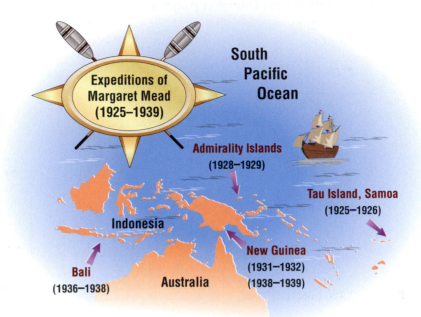

Expeditions of Margaret Mead (1925–1939)

South Pacific Ocean

Admirality Islands (1928–1929)

Tau Island, Samoa (1925–1926)

Indonesia

New Guinea (1931–1932) (1938–1939)

Bali (1936–1938)

Australia

E

Follow-up Activities

1 Refer back to the Prereading Preparation section. Read your description of the work that you thought Margaret Mead did. How accurate was your description?

2 Work with two or three partners. Imagine that you are a team of anthropologists. You are going to a new country to study a different culture. You plan to interview the people there to learn about their culture. What features of this culture do you want to learn about? What questions can you ask to get this information? Together, make a list of questions for your interview. When you are finished, write your questions on the board. Discuss all the groups' questions and, as a class, make up one questionnaire.

3 Use your questionnaire to interview someone from a culture that is different from your own. You may interview someone in your class, but a person outside your class would be better. Bring the answers back to class. Discuss what you learned from your interview.

F Crossword Puzzle

Read the clues on the next page. Write the answers in the correct spaces in the puzzle.

lens

Crossword Puzzle Clues

ACROSS CLUES

1. Margaret Mead went to _college_ at a time when it was not common for women to go to a university.
4. Margaret Mead was a very _popular_ person. Many people knew her and read her books.
7. Margaret Mead was an _____ .
12. Margaret Mead studied different people and their _____ .
13. Because of Margaret Mead, many people became very _int_ in learning about other cultures.
14. American _smoa_ was the first country Margaret Mead went to and studied.
15. Margaret Mead studied many _____ about people's lives, such as what they ate.
16. Margaret Mead learned to _____ other languages.

DOWN CLUES

2. Margaret Mead was interested in other people _____ young women and their lives.
3. Margaret Mead traveled all over the _____ .
5. Margaret Mead wrote many _____ about the cultures she studied.
6. Margaret Mead's first book made her _____ .
8. It is _____ for everyone to understand other people' cultures.
9. Today it is not _____ for women to go to a university to study anthropology.
10. Because of all she did in her life, Margaret Mead was a very _____ woman.
11. The first culture that Margaret Mead studied was very _____ . These people were very gentle.

Cloze Quiz

Read the passage below. Fill in the blanks with the correct words from the list.
Use each word only once.

about	decided	graduated	study
culture	education	learn	

Margaret __graduated__ (1) from college in 1923. She wanted to

continue her __education__ (2) in anthropology, so she __decided__ (3)

to go to American Samoa to __study__ (4) the young women there.

Many people did not know about the __culture__ (5) of American Samoa.

Margaret wanted to learn __about__ (6) Samoans so that the world could

__learn__ (7) about them, too.

because	interested	result	subject
book	popular	returned	wrote

When Margaret __returned__ (8) to the United States from Samoa,

she __wrote__ (9) a book about the young Samoan women she studied.

The __book__ (10) was called *Coming of Age in Samoa,* and it was

very __popular__ (11). As a __result__ (12), Margaret Mead became

very famous. Before Margaret wrote her book, not many people were

__interested__ (13) in anthropology. __because__ (14) of Margaret's book,

anthropology became a popular __subject__ (15), and many people began

to read about different cultures.

CHAPTER 8

Louis Pasteur:
A Modern-Day Scientist

Prereading Preparation

Work with a classmate to discuss these questions.

1. Look at the picture. This man was Louis Pasteur.

   a. What kind of scientific work did he do? What do you think?
   1. He was an inventor.
   2. He was a chemist.
   3. He was a medical doctor.

   b. Where did Louis Pasteur do his work?
   1. In a laboratory
   2. In a hospital
   3. In an office

2. Read the title of this chapter.

   a. How is modern scientific work different from scientific work that people did hundreds of years ago?
   b. Why do you think Louis Pasteur was a modern-day scientist?

Reading

Directions: Read each paragraph carefully. Then answer the questions.

Louis Pasteur: A Modern-Day Scientist

In the summer of 1885, nine-year-old Joseph Meister was a very ill little boy. He had been attacked by a sick dog that had rabies, a deadly disease. His doctor tried to help him, but there was no cure for rabies at that time. The doctor told Joseph's parents that perhaps there was one man who could save Joseph's life. His name was Louis Pasteur.

1 A **disease** is
   a. a summer activity
   b. an attack by an animal
   c. an illness; a sickness

2 What is rabies?

   _____

3 Did Joseph have rabies?
   a. Yes   **b.** No

4 **a.** Was Joseph's doctor able to help him?

   _____

   b. Why or why not?

   _____

5 A **cure** for a disease is
   a. a medicine or treatment that makes an illness go away
   b. a careful description of that disease in a book
   c. a special doctor who knows about that disease

6 **His name was Louis Pasteur.** Who does this refer to?
   a. Joseph's parents
   b. Joseph's doctor
   c. The man who could save Joseph's life

7 What do you think the next paragraph will discuss?

  a. Joseph's life after he became well again

  b. The life of Joseph's doctor

  c. Louis Pasteur's life

When Pasteur was a young boy in France, he was very curious. Louis was especially interested in medicine, so he spent many hours every day with the chemist who lived in his small town. The chemist sold pills, cough syrups, and other types of medicine, just as modern pharmacists, or druggists, do today. At that time, the chemist had to make all the medicines himself. Young Louis enjoyed watching the chemist as he worked and listening to him assist the customers who came to him each day. Pasteur decided that one day he wanted to help people, too.

As a schoolboy, Pasteur worked slowly and carefully. At first, his teachers thought that young Louis might be a slow learner. Through elementary school, high school, and college, Pasteur worked the same thoughtful way. In fact, he was not a slow learner, but a very intelligent young man. He became a college professor and a scientist, and he continued to work very carefully.

8 Louis was **especially** interested in medicine, **so** he spent many hours every day with the chemist who lived in his small town.

  a. Especially means

   1. mostly
   2. probably
   3. originally

  b. So means

   1. because
   2. as a result
   3. all the time

9 Louis was a very **curious** person. He enjoyed watching the chemist as he worked and listening to the chemist **assist** his customers.

  a. Curious means

   1. hardworking
   2. careful
   3. interested in learning

b. **Assist** means

    1. help
    2. sell
    3. work

10 Why did Louis spend many hours with the chemist?

    a. Louis was interested in medicine.
    b. Louis wanted to become a chemist.
    c. The chemist needed Louis's help.

11 The chemist sold pills, cough syrups, and other types of medicine, **just as pharmacists,** or druggists, **do today.**

    a. **Just as** means

        1. only
        2. the same as
        3. whereas

    b. **Pharmacists** are _____

    c. What do pharmacists **do today?**

    _____

12 **As a schoolboy,** Pasteur worked slowly and carefully. **At first,** his teachers thought that young Louis might be a slow learner.

    a. **As a schoolboy** means

        1. Louis acted like a little boy
        2. when Louis was a boy in school
        3. boys in school always work slowly

    b. **At first** means

        1. in the beginning
        2. one time
        3. for one reason

    c. Why did his teacher think Louis might be a slow learner?

    _____

13 _____ True _____ False   Louis was a slow learner and not an intelligent man.

14 _____ True _____ False   Louis continued to work very carefully when he became a professor and a scientist.

15 What do you think the next part of the passage will discuss?

_____

Because of Pasteur's patient methods, he was able to make many observations about germs. For example, germs cause meat and milk to spoil. They also cause many serious diseases. Pasteur was studying about the germs that cause rabies when Joseph Meister became ill. In fact, Pasteur believed he had a cure for rabies, but he had never treated a person with it before. At first, Pasteur was afraid to treat Joseph, but his doctor said the child was dying. Pasteur gave Joseph an inoculation, or shot, every day for ten days. Slowly, the child became better. Pasteur's vaccination cured him.

16 Why was Pasteur able to make many observations about germs?
   a. Because he was very intelligent
   b. Because he was patient
   c. Because germs cause food to spoil

17 Germs cause meat and milk to **spoil.**

   Spoil means
   a. become warm
   b. become inedible
   c. become cold

18 Why was Pasteur afraid to treat Joseph at first?
   a. He had never given the cure to a human before.
   b. He did not think he could cure rabies.
   c. His doctor said the child was dying.

19 Pasteur gave Joseph an **inoculation,** or shot, **every day for ten days.**
   a. What is an **inoculation?**

_____

b. Every day for ten days means

    1. ten shots every day
    2. one shot after ten days
    3. one shot each day for ten days

20 Why did the child become better?

_____

During his lifetime, Pasteur studied germs and learned how they cause diseases in animals and people. He developed vaccinations that prevent many of these illnesses. He also devised the process of pasteurization, which stops food such as milk from spoiling. Louis Pasteur died on September 28, 1895, at the age of 72. Modern medicine continues to benefit from the work of this great scientist.

21 During his lifetime means

    a. in the years that he lived
    b. after he became a college professor
    c. when Joseph Meister was ill

22 Prevent means

    a. describe something carefully
    b. help something happen
    c. stop something from happening

23 What can **vaccinations** do?

    a. Help keep animals and people healthy
    b. Cause illnesses
    c. Stop food from spoiling

24 Pasteur **devised** the **process of pasteurization.**

    a. Devised means

        1. named
        2. invented
        3. liked

    b. A **process** is a

        1. medical treatment
        2. way to make money
        3. specific way of doing something

    c. The **process of pasteurization**

        1. prevents disease

        2. causes illnesses

        3. prevents milk from spoiling

25 **Modern medicine** continues to **benefit** from the work of this great scientist.

    a. **Modern medicine** means

        1. medicine in the past

        2. medicine today

        3. vaccinations

    b. When we **benefit** from something, we

        1. get an advantage

        2. get a disadvantage

Directions: Read the complete passage. When you are finished, answer the questions that follow.

Track 08

Louis Pasteur: A Modern-Day Scientist

1   In the summer of 1885, nine-year-old Joseph Meister was a very ill little boy.
2   He had been attacked by a sick dog that had rabies, a deadly disease. His doctor
3   tried to help him, but there was no cure for rabies at that time. The doctor told
4   Joseph's parents that perhaps there was one man who could save Joseph's life.
5   His name was Louis Pasteur.
6   When Pasteur was a young boy in France, he was very curious. Louis was
7   especially interested in medicine, so he spent many hours every day with the
8   chemist who lived in his small town. The chemist sold pills, cough syrups, and
9   other types of medicine, just as modern pharmacists, or druggists, do today.
10 At that time, the chemist had to make all the medicines himself. Young Louis
11 enjoyed watching the chemist as he worked and listening to him assist the
12 customers who came to him each day. Pasteur decided that one day he wanted
13 to help people, too.

14   As a schoolboy, Pasteur worked slowly and carefully. At first, his teachers
15 thought that young Louis might be a slow learner. Through elementary school,
16 high school, and college, Pasteur worked the same thoughtful way. In fact, he
17 was not a slow learner, but a very intelligent young man. He became a college
18 professor and a scientist, and he continued to work very carefully.

19   Because of Pasteur's patient methods, he was able to make many observations
20 about germs. For example, germs cause meat and milk to spoil. They also cause
21 many serious diseases. Pasteur was studying about the germs that cause rabies
22 when Joseph Meister became ill. In fact, Pasteur believed he had a cure for
23 rabies, but he had never treated a person with it before. At first, Pasteur was
24 afraid to treat Joseph, but his doctor said the child was dying. Pasteur gave
25 Joseph an inoculation, or shot, every day for ten days. Slowly, the child became
26 better. Pasteur's vaccination cured him.

27   During his lifetime, Pasteur studied germs and learned how they cause
28 diseases in animals and people. He developed vaccinations that prevent many
29 of these illnesses. He also devised the process of pasteurization, which stops
30 food such as milk from spoiling. Louis Pasteur died on September 28, 1895,
31 at the age of 72. Modern medicine continues to benefit from the work of this
32 great scientist.

A Scanning for Information

Read the questions. Then go back to the complete passage and scan quickly for the answers. Circle the letter of the correct answer, or write your answer.

1 Why did Pasteur decide he wanted to help people?

_____

_____

2 Why did Pasteur agree to treat Joseph?

_____

_____

3 What were some of Pasteur's observations about germs?

a. _____

b. _____

4 What is the main idea of this story?

    a. Louis Pasteur saved Joseph Meister's life by developing a cure for rabies.

    b. Louis Pasteur was a great scientist whose work continues to help science today.

    c. Louis Pasteur learned about germs and developed the process of pasteurization.

Word Forms

In English, some verbs (v.) become nouns (n.) by dropping the final -e and adding the suffix -tion, for example, graduate (v.), graduation (n.). Read the following sentences. Decide if the word is a noun or a verb. Circle the correct answer.

1 Claire's <u>educates / education</u> included music lessons.
   (v.)   (n.)

2 Claire's parents <u>educated / education</u> her to become a concert violinist.
   (v.)   (n.)

3 In the United States, children need to have certain <u>vaccinates / vaccinations</u> before they begin school.
   (v.)   (n.)

4 In the United States, doctors <u>vaccinate / vaccination</u> children for several serious diseases.
   (v.)   (n.)

5 Paige <u>continued / continuation</u> to study after she graduated from college.
   (v.)   (n.)

6 Paige believed that the <u>continued / continuation</u> of her education was very important.
   (v.)   (n.)

7 Sociologists frequently <u>observe / observation</u> people in public places, such as stores and parks.
   (v.)   (n.)

8 Sociologists record their <u>observe / observations</u> in journals.
   (v.)   (n.)

Word Partnership	Use *observation* with
prep.	by observation, through observation, under observation
adj.	careful observation, direct observation
v.	make an observation

Vocabulary in Context

Read the following sentences. Choose the correct word or phrase for each sentence. Write your answers on the blank lines.

at first	**because of**	**cure** *(n.)*	**decided** *(v.)*

1 Don was very sick last year. _____ his long illness, he missed two months of school.

2 Maria didn't speak English when she came to the United States. _____ , she didn't understand anyone, but gradually, she learned to communicate very well.

3 Last year, Monica _____ to change her job because she wasn't happy with her work.

4 Doctors do not have a _____ for the common cold, but they do for many serious diseases.

assisted *(v.)*	**careful** *(adj.)*	**for example**	**process** *(n.)*

5 Alexandra is always very _____ when she walks across the street. She looks in both directions for cars.

6 Making paper is a simple _____ .

7 The nurse _____ the doctor during the child's medical exam.

8 Modern pharmacies sell many different products in addition to medicine. _____ , they sell magazines, candy, toys, and cards.

caused *(v.)*	curious *(adj.)*	in fact

9 Our college basketball team is very good. _____ , the team lost only one game last year.

10 Cats are very _____ animals. They are interested in looking at everything.

11 Last winter, the ice on the roads _____ many car accidents.

D Topics for Discussion and Writing

1 When Louis Pasteur was a child, he was always interested in medicine. What subject were you interested in when you were a child? Are you still interested in that subject today? Write about this and explain your answer.

2 What medical discovery of the past do you think is the most important? Write a paragraph. Tell why this discovery is important. Describe how it has helped people.

3 Many medical discoveries will be made in the future. What do you think will be the most important cure? Why? Discuss your ideas with your classmates. Decide which cures are the most important. Give your reasons.

4 **Write in your journal.** Think of a time when you or someone you know was not well. Describe the situation. What treatment helped this person? How did it help?

Follow-up Activities

1 Louis Pasteur's discovery of a rabies vaccine saved many lives. What other discoveries help to save lives today? Work in small groups and discuss your ideas. Then complete the chart below. When you are finished, compare your chart with other groups' charts. As a class, discuss these discoveries. Decide which discovery is the most important one.

Discoveries	Illnesses Cured
rabies vaccine	rabies

2 Pasteur developed the process of pasteurization over 100 years ago to make milk safe to drink. Today we know many other ways to prevent food from spoiling. Work with one or two classmates. Talk about some of these ways. Make a list and compare it with your other classmates' lists. Discuss which way is the most important, and why.

Crossword Puzzle

Read the clues on the next page. Write the answers in the correct spaces in the puzzle.

Crossword Puzzle Clues

ACROSS CLUES

2. Pasteur worked slowly and carefully. He was a very ____ man.
3. Some illnesses kill people. These diseases are ____ .
4. After class, the students ____ home.
5. Aspirin and cough syrup are types of ____ .
9. At first, Pasteur did ____ want to inoculate Joseph Meister.
10. Germs cause milk to ____ .
12. People who want to know all about many things are very ____ .
16. Joseph Meister was dying, ____ Pasteur inoculated him, even though he was afraid.
17. Pasteur discovered the ____ for rabies. His vaccination saved many people from rabies.
18. Ill; not well
19. We all ____ from medical discoveries.
20. The past tense of **eat**
21. There is a ____ for rabies.
23. Pasteur did not live in a big city. He lived in a small ____ .
25. Pasteur died ____ 1895.

DOWN CLUES

1. Many people ____ alive today because of Pasteur's vaccine.
2. A ____ , or druggist, prepares medicine.
3. Pasteur ____ his work slowly and carefully.
4. ____ can cause disease.
6. People who shop in stores are called ____ .
7. Each; every
8. We protect ourselves against some diseases with an ____ , or shot.
11. Pasteur was born ____ 1823.
12. We ____ buy medicine in a drugstore, or pharmacy.
13. ____ is a serious disease. We can get it from an animal bite.
14. Pasteur liked to ____ , or help, the druggist.
15. Vaccinations help ____ many kinds of illnesses.
21. Vaccinations are ____ important for children.
22. Pasteur was a professor. He was a scientist, ____ .
24. You and I

Cloze Quiz

Read the following paragraphs. Fill in the blanks with the correct words from the list. Use each word only once.

became	carefully	school	thoughtful
but	learner	scientist	

As a schoolboy, Pasteur always worked slowly and _____ (1).
At first, his teachers thought that young Louis might be a slow

_____ (2). Through elementary school, high _____ (3),
and college, Pasteur worked the same _____ (4) way. In fact, he
was not a slow learner, _____ (5) a very intelligent young man.
He _____ (6) a college professor and a _____ (7), and he
continued to work very carefully.

age	devised	during	studied
benefit	diseases	prevent	such

_____ (8) his lifetime, Pasteur _____ (9) germs and
learned how they cause _____ (10) in animals and people. He
developed vaccinations that _____ (11) many of these illnesses.
He also _____ (12) the process of pasteurization, which stops food
_____ (13) as milk from spoiling. Louis Pasteur died on September
28, 1895, at the _____ (14) of 72. Modern medicine continues to
_____ (15) from the work of this great scientist.

Science and History

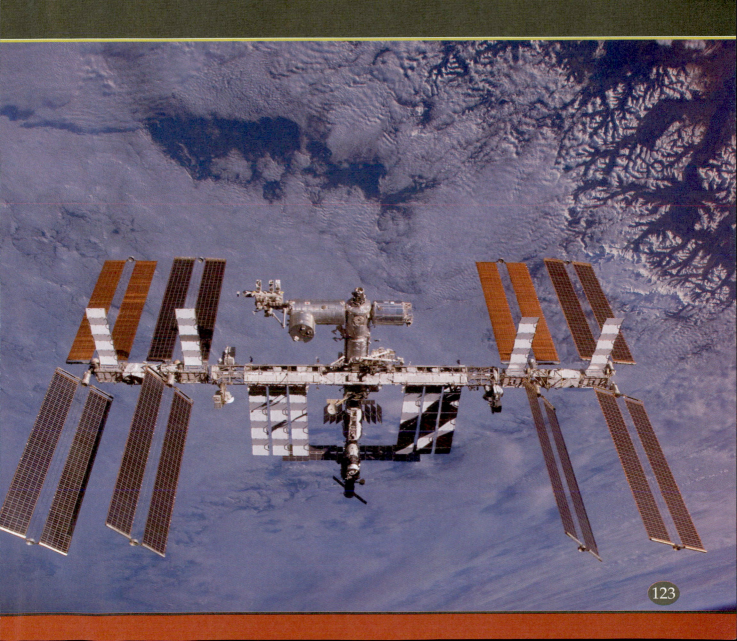

The Origin of the Moon

Prereading Preparation

1 What do you know about the moon? Work with your teacher and your classmates. Try to answer the questions in the chart.

Questions	Answers
How far is the Earth from the moon?	
How old is the moon?	
Does the moon have an atmosphere?	
Where did the moon come from?	
Is there life on the moon?	

Reading

Directions: Read each paragraph carefully. Then answer the questions.

The Origin of the Moon

For thousands of years, people have looked up at the night sky and looked at the moon. They wondered what the moon was made of. They wanted to know how big it was and how far away it was. One of the most interesting questions was "Where did the moon come from?" No one knew for sure. Scientists developed many different theories, or guesses, but they could not prove that their ideas were correct.

Then, between 1969 and 1972, the United States sent astronauts to the moon. They studied the moon and returned to Earth with rock samples. Scientists have studied these pieces of rock, the moon's movements, and information about the moon and the Earth. They can finally answer questions about the origin of the moon.

1 People wondered what the moon was made of.

When people looked at the moon, they felt

   a. curious
   b. afraid
   c. cold

2 _____ True _____ False   Thousands of years ago, people knew how big the moon was.

3 _____ True _____ False   Thousands of years ago, people knew how far away the moon was from the Earth.

4 Scientists developed many different **theories,** or guesses, but they could not prove that their ideas were correct.

   a. A **theory** is
      1. a correct idea
      2. something you already proved
      3. a guess

b. Scientists had

    1. an idea that they were sure about

    2. an idea that they were not sure about

5 Then between 1969 and 1972, the United States sent **astronauts** to the moon.

Astronauts are people who

  a. study rocks

  b. travel in space

  c. live on the moon

6 ____✓____ True _____ False   Scientists now think that they know the origin of the moon.

7 What do you think the next paragraph will discuss?

_____

Today most scientists believe that the moon formed from the Earth. They think that a large object hit the Earth early in its history. Perhaps the object was as big as Mars. When the object hit the Earth, huge pieces of the Earth broke off. These pieces went into orbit around the Earth. After a brief time, the pieces came together and formed the moon.

This "impact theory" explains many facts about the Earth and the moon. For example, the moon is very dry because the impact created so much heat that it dried up all the water. The Earth has iron in its center. However, the moon has very little iron in its center. This is because the moon formed from lighter materials that make up the outer part of the Earth. Finally, the Earth and the moon are almost the same age—the Earth is about 4.5 billion years old, and the moon is about 4.4 billion years old.

8 **Scientists think that a large object hit the Earth early in its history.**

When the object hit the Earth,

  a. people saw it happen

  b. the Earth was new

  c. people wrote about it

UNIT 5   SCIENCE AND HISTORY

9 These pieces went into **orbit** around the Earth.

An **orbit** is

a. a path or route around something in space
b. a large distance in space
c. a large rock in space

10 The moon is very dry because the **impact** created so much heat that it dried up all the water.

An **impact** happens when

a. an object moves past another object
b. an object hits another object

11 Scientists believe that in the past,

a. the moon was part of the Earth
b. the moon was close to Mars
c. the moon hit the Earth

12 Scientists believe that

a. the moon was always in one piece
b. the moon is made up of many big pieces

13 **The astronauts brought back pieces of rock from the moon.**

It is probably true that

a. the rock from the moon is just like rock on Earth
b. the rock from the moon is different from rock on Earth

14 The **impact theory** describes

a. scientists' beliefs about the size of the Earth and Mars
b. scientists' beliefs about the origin of the moon

15 How many facts about the Earth and the moon are in the second paragraph on page 126?

a. Two
b. Three
c. Four

16 Which statement is true?

a. The Earth is 4.5 billion years old, and the moon is, too.
b. The moon is 4.5 billion years old, but the Earth isn't.
c. The Earth is 4.5 billion years old, but the moon isn't.

No one can <u>prove</u> that something really happened billions of years ago. In the future, new information will either support this theory or show that it is wrong. For now, scientists <u>accept</u> the "impact theory" because it explains what we know today about the Earth and the moon.

17 _____ True _____✓_____ False   Scientists are sure that their idea is correct.

18 In the future, **new information will either support this theory or show that it is wrong.**

Information that supports the scientists' theory
  a. helps prove the theory is correct
  b. helps prove the theory is wrong

19 **Scientists accept the impact theory** because
  a. no one can prove that the impact theory isn't true
  b. the information they have about the Earth and the moon supports the impact theory

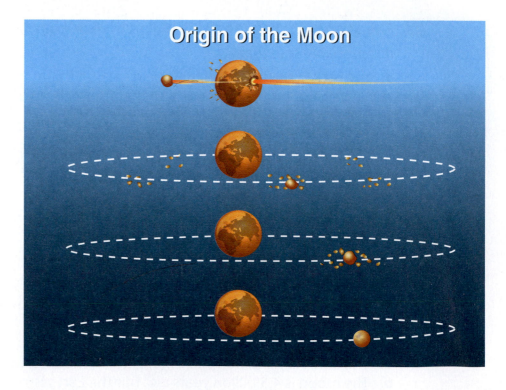

Origin of the Moon

UNIT 5   SCIENCE AND HISTORY

Directions: Read the complete passage. When you are finished, answer the questions that follow.

The Origin of the Moon

1 For thousands of years, people have looked up at the night sky and looked at
2 the moon. They wondered what the moon was made of. They wanted to know
3 how big it was and how far away it was. One of the most interesting questions
4 was "Where did the moon come from?" No one knew for sure. Scientists
5 developed many different theories, or guesses, but they could not prove that
6 their ideas were correct.
7 Then, between 1969 and 1972, the United States sent astronauts to the moon.
8 They studied the moon and returned to Earth with rock samples. Scientists have
9 studied these pieces of rock, the moon's movements, and information about
10 the moon and the Earth. They can finally answer questions about the origin
11 of the moon.
12 Today most scientists believe that the moon formed from the Earth. They
13 think that a large object hit the Earth early in its history. Perhaps the object was
14 as big as Mars. When the object hit the Earth, huge pieces of the Earth broke off.
15 These pieces went into orbit around the Earth. After a brief time, the pieces came
16 together and formed the moon.
17 This "impact theory" explains many facts about the Earth and the moon. For
18 example, the moon is very dry because the impact created so much heat that
19 it dried up all the water. The Earth has iron in its center. However, the moon
20 has very little iron in its center. This is because the moon formed from lighter
21 materials that make up the outer part of the Earth. Finally, the Earth and the
22 moon are almost the same age—the Earth is about 4.5 billion years old, and the
23 moon is about 4.4 billion years old.
24 No one can prove that something really happened billions of years ago. In the
25 future, new information will either support this theory or show that it is wrong.
26 For now, scientists accept the "impact theory" because it explains what we know
27 today about the Earth and the moon.

Scanning for Information

Read the questions. Then go back to the complete passage and scan quickly for the answers. Circle the letter of the correct answer, or write your answer.

1 **a.** How many times did the United States send astronauts to the moon?

  1. One time
  2. Three times
  3. We don't know.

  b. What did the astronauts bring back with them?

  _____

2 What kinds of information did scientists study in order to explain the origin of the moon?

  _____

  _____

  _____

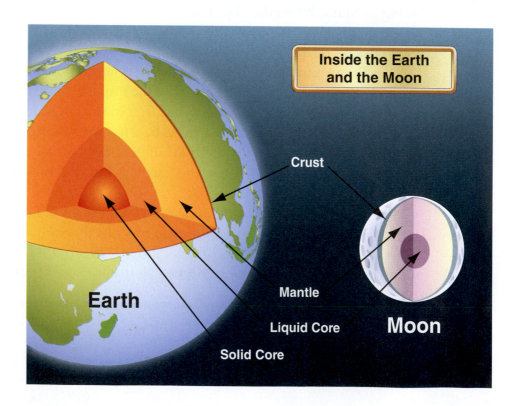

Inside the Earth and the Moon

Crust

Earth

Mantle

Liquid Core   **Moon**

Solid Core

3 **a.** Describe the **impact theory.**

_____

_____

b. What are some facts about the Earth and the moon that this theory explains?

_____

_____

c. How will future information affect this theory?

_____

_____

4 What is the main idea of this story?

a. The Earth and the moon are the same age.

b. The "impact theory" is the best explanation of the moon's origin for several reasons.

c. Scientists have developed different theories to explain the origin of the moon.

B

Word Forms

In English, some verbs (v.) become nouns (n.) by adding the suffix *-tion*, for example, *educate* (v.), *education* (n.). Sometimes there are spelling changes, too. Read the sentences. Decide if each sentence needs a noun or a verb. Circle the correct answer.

1 The librarian <u>informed / information</u> me that the library is not open
on Sunday.   (v.)   (n.)

2 She gave me this <u>informed / information</u> over the telephone
yesterday morning. (v.)   (n.)

3 Scientists believe that the <u>formed / formation</u> of the Earth and Mars happened at the same time. (v.)   (n.)

4 The Earth and Mars <u>formed / formation</u> at the same time.
(v.)   (n.)

5 Drug companies frequently <u>create / creation</u> new medicines.
(v.)   (n.)

6 The <u>create / creation</u> of these new medicines takes a long time.
(v.)   (n.)

7 Our teacher always <u>explains / explanations</u> the directions very clearly.
(v.)   (n.)

8 We usually understand her <u>explains / explanations</u>.
(v.)   (n.)

Word Partnership	Use *explanation* with
adj.	**brief** explanation, **detailed** explanation, **logical** explanation, **only** explanation, **possible** explanation
v.	**give an** explanation, **offer an** explanation, **provide an** explanation

C

Vocabulary in Context

Read the sentences. Choose the correct word or phrase for each sentence. Write your answers on the blank lines.

development (n.)	support (v.)	theory (n.)	wonder (v.)

1 Henry told me his _____ about the origin of all the planets.

2 Many people _____ if there is life on other planets, such as Mars.

3 The ______________ of useful theories is very important.

4 Some scientific tests ______________ Albert Einstein's theories about time.

6	5	7
for now	**in the future**	**then**

5 Travel to Mars is not possible right now, but ______________ astronauts may travel to Mars or other planets.

6 Matt is only 14, so he rides his bicycle to school ______________. However, when he is 17, he will be able to drive a car to school.

7 I bought Kim a gift for her birthday. ______________ I went to her home and gave it to her.

9	8	10 maybe
but *(conj.)*	**finally** *(adv.)*	**perhaps**

8 We wanted to go on vacation, but we didn't have enough money. We saved our money for two years, and we were ______________ able to take a long vacation.

9 Max called Joyce on the telephone last night, ______________ she wasn't home. He'll try to speak with her again today.

10 I don't know the directions to the bank. ______________ my sister can give you that information. She knows the city very well.

Topics for Discussion and Writing

1 Do you think it is important to study the moon and the planets? Why or why not? Write a paragraph to explain your reasons.

Mars

2 In the past, only astronauts went into space. Today, however, other people can go into space, too. Do you want to go into space? Why or why not? Discuss your answer with your classmates.

3 Today most scientists believe that the moon formed from the Earth. They think that a large object hit the Earth early in its history. This is called the "impact theory." Write a letter to a friend and explain the "impact theory." Use your own words.

4 **Write in your journal.** Some groups of people believe that there may be life on other planets. They are searching for signs of life. Do you agree that there may be life on other planets? Why or why not?

Follow-up Activities

1 Work with two or three people. Your group is going to send a spacecraft into space. Decide where it will go. Why do you want the spacecraft to go there? What do you want to find out about this place? Write your group's plan on the board. Compare all the groups' plans. As a class, vote on which plan is best.

2 Some countries, such as the United States and Russia, are planning to build space stations on the planet Mars. People will live and work there. Work with a group. Discuss the advantages and disadvantages of living on Mars. Make a list of both, and compare your list with the other groups' lists. Decide if it is a good idea to send people to Mars to live and work.

Crossword Puzzle

Read the clues on the next page. Write the answers in the correct spaces in the puzzle.

Crossword Puzzle Clues

3. Scientists _____ the moon came from the Earth, but they do not have proof.
5. Scientists study the _____ of the moon around the Earth.
6. The sun is very _____, but the Earth is not.
7. The opposite of **no**
9. The moon is the brightest _____ in the night sky.
10. The opposite of **yes**
12. When we look _____ at the sky, we see the sun, the stars, the moon, and planets.
13. The distance _____ the Earth to the moon is about 250,000 miles.
15. New information may _____, or help prove, the scientists' belief.
18. The scientists may be _____, or incorrect.
19. Many scientists believe that the moon was _____ from the Earth.
22. The past tense of **put**
23. People have several _____, or guesses, about the origin of the moon.
26. When a rock hits something hard, it can break into _____.
27. Astronomers are _____ who study the stars and planets.
29. The Earth and the moon are both about 4.5 _____ years old.

1. The Earth has iron in its _____, or middle.
2. Scientists _____ a lot of information about the Earth and the moon.
3. Scientists believe that a large object hit the Earth and _____ into many pieces.
4. Scientists need more _____ about the Earth and the moon.
5. The Earth has one _____, but Mars has two.
6. Scientists believe that a large object _____ the Earth many millions of years ago.
8. We need a lot of information in order to _____ something that happened a long time ago.
11. The path, or route, that the moon takes around the Earth is called an _____.
14. When one object hits another object, it _____, or makes, heat.
15. **He, _____, it**

16. Scientists cannot _____ their theory. They can only say that evidence supports it.
17. Maybe; possibly
20. When an object hits something, this is called an _____.
21. People look up _____ the moon and think about it.
24. Scientists ask questions about the _____ of the moon. They also ask how the Earth was formed.
25. The present tense of **ate**
28. The _____ is the brightest object in the sky during the day.
30. The Earth _____ the only planet we know that has life.

Cloze Quiz

Read the following paragraphs. Fill in the blanks with the correct words from the list. Use each word only once.

around	facts	moon	time
believe	heat	object	
dry	large	pieces	

Today most scientists _____(1)_____ that the moon formed from the Earth. They think that a _____(2)_____ object hit the Earth. Perhaps the _____(3)_____ was as big as Mars. When the object hit the Earth, huge _____(4)_____ of the Earth broke off. These pieces went into orbit _____(5)_____ the Earth. After a brief _____(6)_____, the pieces came together and formed the _____(7)_____. This "impact theory" explains many _____(8)_____ about the Earth and the moon. For example, the moon is very _____(9)_____ because the impact created so much _____(10)_____ that it dried up all the water.

center	future	same	wrong
Earth	however	scientists	
either	prove	theory	

The Earth has iron in its center. _____ (11) , the moon has very little iron in its _____ (12) . The moon formed from lighter materials that make up the outer part of the _____ (13) . Finally, the Earth and the moon are almost the _____ (14) age—about 4.5 billion years old.

No one can _____ (15) that something really happened billions of years ago. In the _____ (16) , new information will _____ (17) support this theory or show that it is _____ (18) . For now, _____ (19) accept the impact _____ (20) because it explains what we know about the Earth and the moon.

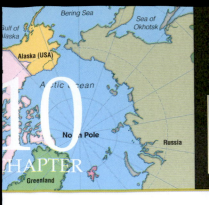

A New Route across the Top of the World

The New Ocean Route between Europe and Asia

Prereading Preparation

1 Look at the map above. Where does this trip begin? _____

Where does this trip end? _____

2 How do people travel on this route?
  a. By plane
  b. By ship
  c. By train

3 Read the title of this story and look at the map.
  a. Why do you think this is a **new** route?

  _____

  b. Which ocean is at the **top of the world?**

  _____

Reading

Directions: Read each paragraph carefully. Then answer the questions.

A New Route across the Top of the World

For the first time in history, the most direct shipping route between Europe and Asia is clear of ice. The Northeast Passage, which connects the Atlantic Ocean and the Pacific Ocean, used to be covered in ice all year. In the past, ships could not travel in this direction because of all the ice. However, the ice cover has steadily decreased, so now travel is possible.

1 A **route** is

   a. a direction

   b. a large boat

   c. an ocean

2 **Clear of ice** means

   a. there is only a little ice

   b. there is no ice

   c. the ice is very clear

3 What two oceans does the Northeast Passage connect?

_____

4 In the past, ships could not travel in the Northeast Passage. Why not?

   a. It was a difficult trip.

   b. It was covered in ice.

   c. It was too long.

5 The ice cover has steadily **decreased.**

   Decreased means

   a. became larger

   b. stayed the same size

   c. became smaller

6 Can ships travel in the Northeast Passage now? _____ Yes _____ No

The Northeast Passage is a shortcut between Europe and Asia through the Canadian Arctic. Part of the Arctic sea ice melts each summer and freezes again in the winter. Still, too much ice covered the sea, even in the summer. Over the last several years, the ice cover has decreased. This shrinking is a result of global warming. Global warming is the increase in the average temperature of the Earth's near-surface air and oceans since the 1950s. Scientists report that the Arctic Ocean ice cap has decreased to its lowest levels in the past few summers.

7 The Northeast Passage is a **shortcut** from Europe to Asia through the Canadian Arctic.

What does **shortcut** mean?

a. A faster way to do something
b. A longer way to do something
c. A new way to do something

8 **Over the last several years, the ice cover has decreased.**

Why did this happen?

a. Global warming makes temperatures higher.
b. Global warming makes temperatures lower.

9 This **shrinking** is a result of global warming.

Shrinking means to

a. get a result
b. increase in size
c. decrease in size

10 Scientists report that the Arctic Ocean **ice cap** shrank to its lowest levels in the past few summers.

This **ice cap** is

a. ice on top of a mountain
b. ice on top of a ship
c. ice on top of an ocean

CHAPTER 10   A NEW ROUTE ACROSS THE TOP OF THE WORLD

Two German ships were the first to cross the Arctic's Northeast Passage. They traveled from Ulsan, South Korea, to Yamburg, Siberia. Traditionally, shippers traveling from Asia to Europe had to go through the Gulf of Aden and through the Suez Canal into the Mediterranean Sea and then into the Atlantic Ocean. Using that traditional route, a journey from South Korea to the Netherlands, for example, is about 12,700 miles. However, the same route through the Northeast Passage is approximately 9,200 miles. It is a lot faster, too—about ten days shorter. This not only saves time, but also saves fuel.

11 **Traditionally** means
- **a.** in the past
- **b.** now
- **c.** recently

12 If you are traveling from South Korea to Siberia, which trip takes longer?
- **a.** A journey through the Northeast Passage
- **b.** A journey through the Suez Canal

The opening of the passage is already causing disagreements among several countries. Canada says that it wants to control the parts of the Northeast Passage that go through its country. The United States and many European countries disagree. They believe that the new route is an international passage and that any ship can use it.

In the future, the route may become even more open. However, scientists don't believe that it will be open year-round because weather patterns sometimes change. This could freeze the passage up again for long periods of time.

13 What do several countries disagree about?
- **a.** When to use the Northeast Passage
- **b.** Who controls the Northeast Passage
- **c.** How long the Northeast Passage is open

14 In the future, the **route** may become even more open.
What is the **route?**

_____

UNIT 5   SCIENCE AND HISTORY

15 Scientists don't believe that the Northeast Passage will be open **year-round.**

What does **year-round** mean?

a. Only in the summer months
b. Only in the winter months
c. All 12 months of the year

16 **Scientists don't believe that the Northeast Passage will be open year-round.**

Why not?

a. The route is very crowded.
b. The water may freeze up again.
c. It's a very long route.

Directions: Read the complete passage. When you are finished, answer the questions that follow.

Track 10

A New Route across the Top of the World

1   For the first time in history, the most direct shipping route between Europe
2   and Asia is clear of ice. The Northeast Passage, which connects the Atlantic
3   Ocean and the Pacific Ocean, used to be covered in ice all year. In the past, ships
4   could not travel this route because of all the ice. However, the ice cover has
5   steadily decreased, so now travel is possible.
6   The Northeast Passage is a shortcut between Europe and Asia through the
7   Canadian Arctic. Part of the Arctic sea ice melts each summer before freezing
8   again in the winter. Still, too much ice covered the sea, even in the summer. Over
9   the last several years, the ice cover has decreased. This shrinking is a result of
10 global warming. Global warming is the increase in the average temperature of
11 the Earth's near-surface air and oceans since the 1950s. Scientists report that the
12 Arctic Ocean ice cap has decreased to its lowest levels in the past few summers.
13   Two German ships were the first to cross the Arctic's Northeast Passage.
14 They traveled from Ulsan, South Korea, to Yamburg, Siberia. Traditionally,

shippers traveling between Asia and Europe had to go through the Gulf of
Aden and through the Suez Canal into the Mediterranean Sea and then into
the Atlantic Ocean. Using that traditional route, a journey from South Korea to
the Netherlands, for example, is about 12,700 miles. However, the same route
through the Northeast Passage is only approximately 9,200 miles. It is a lot
faster, too—about ten days shorter. This not only saves time, but also saves fuel.

The opening of the passage is already causing disagreements among several
countries. Canada says that it wants to control the parts of the Northeast Passage
that go through its country. The United States and many European countries
disagree. They believe that the new route is an international passage and that
any ship can use it.

In the future, the route may become even more open. However, scientists
don't believe that it will be open year-round because weather patterns sometimes
change. This could freeze the passage up again for long periods of time.

View of the North Pole Area of the Earth

UNIT 5   SCIENCE AND HISTORY

Scanning for Information

Read the questions. Then go back to the complete passage and scan quickly for the answers. Write your answer in the space provided.

1 What is the Northeast Passage?

_____

_____

2 Why is travel on this route possible today?

_____

_____

3 What has caused this to happen?

_____

_____

4 What was the route of the first ships to use this passage?

_____

_____

5 What are the advantages of this new route?

_____

_____

6 What do several countries disagree about?

_____

_____

Word Forms

In English, some words can be either a noun (n.) or a verb (v.), for example, *cause*. Read the sentences below. Decide if the correct word is a noun or a verb. Circle your answer.

1. <u>Travel / travel</u> to another country can be very expensive.
      (n.)   (v.)

2. Every summer, I <u>travel / travel</u> to Mexico with my family.
               (n.)   (v.)

3. Many large <u>ships / ships</u> cross the Pacific Ocean every day.
            (n.)   (v.)

4. My uncle's company <u>ships / ships</u> heavy equipment from the U.S. to Mexico.
                 (n.)   (v.)

5. A meteorologist <u>reports / reports</u> the weather on the news every morning.
              (n.)   (v.)

6. I always listen to several news <u>reports / reports</u> before I leave for school.
                      (n.)   (v.)

7. The temperature in the U.S. <u>increases / increases</u> in the spring and summer.
                 (n.)   (v.)

8. There is an <u>increase / increase</u> in the number of students in my class this year.
         (n.)   (v.)

9. Heat <u>causes / causes</u> ice to melt.
      (n.)   (v.)

10. Heavy rain or snow are often the <u>cause / cause</u> of traffic accidents.
                  (n.)   (v.)

Word Partnership	Use *increase* with
adv.	increase **dramatically**, increase **rapidly**
n.	**population** increase, **price** increase, **salary** increase, increase **in crime**, increase **in demand**, increase **in spending**, increase **in temperature**, increase **in value**
adj.	**big** increase, **marked** increase, **sharp** increase

Vocabulary in Context

Read the following sentences. Choose the correct word or phrase for each sentence. Write your answers on the blank lines.

route (n.)	**shortcut** (n.)	**temperature** (n.)

1 The distance from Robert's house to his friend's house is three miles, but if he takes a _____, the distance is only two miles.

2 What is the quickest _____ from the library to the college? I'm in a hurry.

3 Many people are most comfortable when the _____ is about 65° Fahrenheit.

cause (v.)	**freeze** (v.)	**shrink** (v.)

4 If I wash my sweater in hot water, it will _____. I need to wash it in cold water.

5 Will increasing temperatures _____ the ice to melt at the South Pole, too?

6 I like to _____ fresh vegetables. Then I can eat them whenever I want.

| decrease (v.) | global warming (n.) | melt (v.) | traditionally (adv.) |

7 There are many causes of _____. One cause is the burning of coal and oil.

8 _____, most Americans have a cake on their birthday.

9 That chocolate will _____ if you leave it on the table in the sun.

10 You need to _____ the amount of water you are giving the flowers. Too much water will harm them.

D

Topics for Discussion and Writing

1 The ice in the Arctic Ocean is melting because of global warming. Do you think this increase in temperature affects the animals that live in the Arctic? How?

2 What do you think are some causes of global warming? Discuss some possible reasons with your classmates.

3 Some companies use ships to transport their products. Why do you think they use ships instead of airplanes? Discuss some possible reasons with your classmates.

4 **Write in your journal.** Do you think global warming is dangerous to the environment? Why or why not? Explain your reasons and give examples.

Follow-up Activities

Look at the map below. Answer the questions that follow.

Ocean Routes between Europe and Asia

The new route between Europe and Asia
The traditional ocean route between Europe and Asia

1 What is the distance from Yokohama to Rotterdam using the southerly route? _____ miles

2 What is the distance from Yokohama to Rotterdam using the Northeast Passage? _____ miles

3 Which route is shorter? _____

4 Why is it shorter? _____

_____

5 What are some advantages of a shorter route? _____

_____

Crossword Puzzle

Read the clues on the next page. Write the answers in the correct spaces in the puzzle.

Crossword Puzzle Clues

7. The _____ outside is 65 degrees.
8. I enjoy traveling by _____. I love the ocean!
10. You can _____ your strength by exercising every day.
11. I _____ swim very well.
12. Many scientists worry that _____ warming will cause the ocean level to rise.
15. The children took a _____ across the park to get home.
18. Our family has _____ had New Year's Day dinner at five o'clock, but this year we will eat at seven o'clock.
20. A _____ is a drawing of a city, a country, or even the whole world.

1. Voyage; journey
2. Water will _____ at 32° Fahrenheit.
3. Here are the directions to my house. It is a very direct _____.
4. The past tense of **give**
5. When fall turns into winter, the temperature will _____.
6. If you wash that sweater in hot water, it will _____. Then it will not fit you anymore.
9. The opposite of **no**
11. Very cold weather can _____ your skin to become red.
13. The _____ Ocean is at the top of the world.
14. The newspapers will _____ on the accident in tomorrow's paper.
16. The opposite of **big**
17. Butter will _____ if you put it on a hot dish.
19. Your hair is on _____ of your head.

G

Cloze Quiz

Read the following paragraphs. Fill in the blanks with the correct words from the list. Use each word only once.

air	lowest	result	years
between	melts	sea	
increase	report	winter	

The Northeast Passage is a shortcut _____ (1) Europe and Asia through the Canadian Arctic. Part of the Arctic sea ice _____ (2) each summer before freezing again in the _____ (3). Still, too much ice covered the _____ (4), even in the summer. Over the last several _____ (5), the ice cover has decreased. This shrinking is a _____ (6) of global warming. Global warming is the _____ (7) in the average temperature of the Earth's near-surface _____ (8) and oceans since the 1950s. Scientists _____ (9) that the Arctic Ocean ice cap has decreased to its _____ (10) levels in the past few summers.

approximately	faster	saves	traveled
cross	route	through	
example	same	traditionally	

Two German ships were the first to _____ (11) the Arctic's Northeast Passage. They _____ (12) from Ulsan, South Korea, to Yamburg, Siberia. _____ (13), shippers traveling from Asia to Europe

had to go through the Gulf of Aden and _____ the Suez Canal
(14)
into the Mediterranean Sea and then into the Atlantic Ocean. Using that
traditional _____, a journey from South Korea to the Netherlands,
(15)
for _____, is about 12,700 miles. However, the _____
(16)   (17)
route through the Northeast Passage is _____ 9,200 miles. It is a
(18)
lot _____, too—about 10 days shorter. This not only saves time,
(19)
but also _____ fuel.
(20)

Future Technology Today

11 CHAPTER

Saving Lives with Weather Forecasting

Prereading Preparation

1 What is weather forecasting? Who does it?

_____

2 Look at the photograph. Work with a partner. What do you think happens to buildings when a tornado strikes?

_____

3 Read the title of this chapter. What do you think this story will discuss?

_____

Reading

Directions: Read each paragraph carefully. Then answer the questions.

Saving Lives with Weather Forecasting

On the night of April 25, 1994, a massive tornado struck the town of Lancaster, Texas. The tornado destroyed more than 175 homes. It also flattened the business district. Ordinarily, a tornado like the one that struck Lancaster kills dozens of people. Amazingly, only four people died.

1 **Massive** means
   a. destroy
   b. very big
   c. windy

2 ____ True ____ False   The tornado destroyed the business district.

3 **Ordinarily** means
   a. usually
   b. really
   c. obviously

4 **Amazingly, only four people died.**

This sentence means
   a. it is good that only four people died
   b. it is surprising that only four people died
   c. it is sad that four people died

Why did so few people die that night in Lancaster? Part of the reason is modern weather technology: Next Generation Weather Radar, or Nexrad. This sphere-shaped instrument identified the tornado a full 40 minutes before the tornado hit. As a result, weather forecasters were able to warn the people in the town. This advance warning helped many people to leave Lancaster before the tornado struck.

Nexrad is the first weather-service radar system that can detect strong winds and rain, which are characteristics of severe thunderstorms and tornadoes. In the past, a now-obsolete radar system was used to predict such storms. Under this old system, warnings often depended on eyewitness reports. These reports gave people only about three minutes to prepare for the tornado.

5 What is Nexrad?

_____

6 This **advance warning** helped many people to leave Lancaster before the tornado struck.

Advance warning means

a. warning people before something happens
b. warning people after something happens

7 ___✓___ True _____ False   Two characteristics of thunderstorms and tornadoes are wind and rain.

8 **Characteristic** means

a. wind or rain
b. reason or cause
c. quality or trait

9 In the past, a now-**obsolete** radar system was used to predict such storms.

Obsolete means

a. not useful
b. very new
c. very useful

Today, there are 159 Nexrad systems in the United States. Before Nexrad, many severe thunderstorms and tornadoes struck without warning. Weather forecasters could not predict all of them. Now, Nexrad predicts more than 60 percent of all tornadoes. Because of this, weather forecasters can tell people ahead of time so that they can prepare for a tornado. As a result, the number of people who die in tornadoes in the U.S. decreased by 50 percent. In other words, this number was cut in half!

10 What percent of all tornadoes does Nexrad predict?

    a. 159 percent

    b. 50 percent

    c. 60 percent

11 How many Nexrad systems are there in the United States? _159_

12 As a result, the number of people who die in tornadoes in the United States **decreased** by 50 percent.

    Decrease means

    a. become higher

    b. become lower

    c. stay the same

Tornadoes occur all over the world, but most often in the United States. One-third of all U.S. tornadoes strike in Oklahoma, Texas, and Kansas. Alaska is the only state that has never had a tornado. A tornado may last from several seconds to several hours, and its winds may reach up to 300 miles per hour (500 kilometers per hour). Because tornadoes are so powerful and so destructive, it is important to be able to predict them accurately. Consequently, the Nexrad system is an indispensable part of American weather forecasting.

13 _____ True __✓__ False   Tornadoes occur only in the United States.

14 __✓__ True _____ False   Tornadoes may last a short time or a long time.

15 Because tornadoes are so powerful and so destructive, it is important to be able to predict them **accurately.**

Accurately means

a. exactly
b. carefully
c. early

16 **Consequently,** the Nexrad system is an **indispensable** part of American weather forecasting.

a. **Consequently** means

1. however
2. as a result
3. hopefully

b. **Indispensable** means

1. useful
2. new
3. necessary

UNIT 6 FUTURE TECHNOLOGY TODAY

Reading

Directions: Read the complete passage. When you are finished, answer the questions that follow.

Track 11

Saving Lives with Weather Forecasting

1   On the night of April 25, 1994, a massive tornado struck the town of Lancaster,
2   Texas. The tornado destroyed more than 175 homes. It also flattened the business
3   district. Ordinarily, a tornado like the one that struck Lancaster kills dozens of
4   people. Amazingly, only four people died.

5   Why did so few people die that night in Lancaster? Part of the reason is modern
6   weather technology: Next Generation Weather Radar, or Nexrad. This sphere-
7   shaped instrument identified the tornado a full 40 minutes before the tornado hit.
8   As a result, weather forecasters were able to warn the people in the town. This
9   advance warning helped many people to leave Lancaster before the tornado struck.

10   Nexrad is the first weather-service radar system that can detect strong winds
11   and rain, which are characteristics of severe thunderstorms and tornadoes. In the
12   past, a now-obsolete radar system was used to predict such storms. Under this
13   old system, warnings often depended on eyewitness reports. These reports gave
14   people only about three minutes to prepare for the tornado.

15   Today, there are 159 Nexrad systems in the United States. Before Nexrad,
16   many severe thunderstorms and tornadoes struck without warning. Weather
17   forecasters could not predict all of them. Now, Nexrad predicts more than
18   60 percent of all tornadoes. Because of this, weather forecasters can tell people
19   ahead of time so that they can prepare for a tornado. As a result, the number of
20   people who die in tornadoes in the U.S. decreased by 50 percent. In other words,
21   this number was cut in half!

22   Tornadoes occur all over the world, but most often in the United States.
23   One-third of all U.S. tornadoes strike in Oklahoma, Texas, and Kansas. Alaska
24   is the only state that has never had a tornado. A tornado may last from several
25   seconds to several hours, and its winds may reach up to 300 miles per hour
26   (500 kilometers per hour). Because tornadoes are so powerful and so destructive,
27   it is important to be able to predict them accurately. Consequently, the Nexrad
28   system is an indispensable part of American weather forecasting.

Scanning for Information

Read the questions. Then go back to the complete passage and scan quickly for the answers. Circle the letter of the correct answer, or write your answer.

1 Read line 4. Why was it amazing that only four people died?

_____

_____

2 How does Nexrad save lives?

_____

_____

3 Before Nexrad, how did many forecasters know that a tornado was coming?

_____

_____

4 Is it important to accurately predict tornadoes? Why or why not?

_____

_____

5 What is the main idea of this story?

   a. Tornadoes occur all over the world, but most tornadoes strike the United States.

   b. There is a new weather system that can predict tornadoes and save lives.

   c. A massive tornado struck a town in Texas, but only four people died.

B Word Forms

In English, some verbs (v.) become nouns (n.) by adding *-ence* or *-ance*. Read the sentences below. Decide if each sentence needs a verb or a noun. Circle the correct answer.

1 Carmen <u>avoided / avoidance</u> caffeine while she was pregnant.
       (v.)   *(n.)*

2 <u>Avoid / Avoidance</u> of caffeine is important for a healthy baby.
       (v.)   *(n.)*

3 Joanne's <u>depends / dependence</u> on her car is a problem.
            (v.)   *(n.)*

4 Joanne <u>depends / dependence</u> on her car to drive only three blocks to the store.
         (v.)   *(n.)*

5 Some buildings <u>resist / resistance</u> high winds.
                  (v.)   *(n.)*

6 This wind <u>resist / resistance</u> can save lives during a tornado.
            (v.)   *(n.)*

7 Tornadoes are a rare <u>occur / occurrence</u> in New Jersey.
                       (v.)   *(n.)*

8 They rarely <u>occur / occurrence</u> in Hawaii.
              (v.)   *(n.)*

Word Partnership	Use *occur* with
n.	**accidents** occur, **changes** occur, **deaths** occur, **diseases** occur, **events** occur, **injuries** occur, **problems** occur
adv.	**frequently** occur, **naturally** occur, **normally** occur, **often** occur, **usually** occur

Vocabulary in Context

Read the sentences. Choose the correct word for each sentence. Write your answers on the blank lines.

| indispensable (adj.) | obsolete (adj.) | severe (adj.) |

1 Because most businesses use computers, typewriters have become __obsolete__ .

2 Computers are __indispensable__ to most businesses. Without them, businesses could not operate!

3 Danielle has a __severe__ cold. Her doctor told her to stay in bed for several days.

| accurately (adv.) | amazingly (adv.) | consequently (adv.) |

4 Kristen did not study last night. __Consequently__ , she was not prepared for the exam this morning.

5 My wristwatch keeps time __accurately__ . It is now exactly noon.

6 I saw a terrible car accident on the highway. __amazingly__ , no one was hurt.

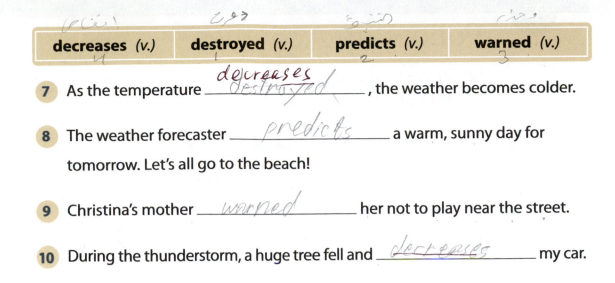

decreases (v.)	destroyed (v.)	predicts (v.)	warned (v.)

7 As the temperature _decreases destroyed_, the weather becomes colder.

8 The weather forecaster _predicts_ a warm, sunny day for tomorrow. Let's all go to the beach!

9 Christina's mother _warned_ her not to play near the street.

10 During the thunderstorm, a huge tree fell and _decreases_ my car.

D Topics for Discussion and Writing

1 Nexrad is an important system because it can save lives. Think about another invention (for example, a smoke detector) that can save lives. Describe this invention. What does it do? Write a paragraph about it.

2 Many people listen to the weather forecast every day. Do you listen to it? Why or why not? Do you think listening to the weather forecast is necessary every day? Write a paragraph about this.

3 How can you prepare for severe weather? What items can you keep in your home in case there is severe weather, such as a hurricane or a snowstorm? Work with a partner and prepare a list together.

4 **Write in your journal.** Did you ever experience severe weather (tornadoes, snowstorms, floods, etc.)? Write about this experience. If you did not experience bad weather yourself, write about what you read in a newspaper or heard about on television or on the radio.

Take just 1 topic and write programph.

Follow-up Activities

1 Study the four illustrations carefully. Then put the four steps below the illustrations in the correct order. Number them 1 to 4.

How a Tornado Is Formed

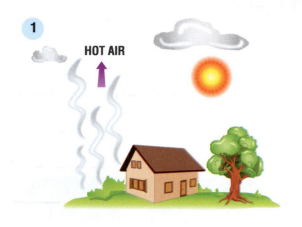

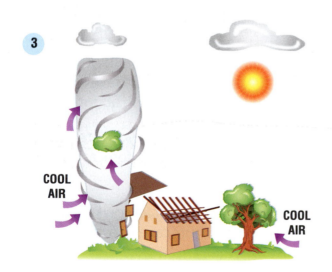

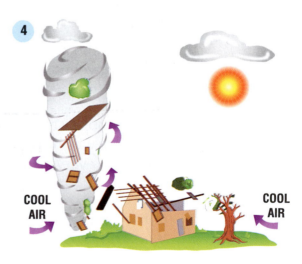

_____ Cooler air nearby rushes in to fill the space left by the rising hot air.

_____ As the Earth rotates, it causes a rotating motion in the air column. This process becomes stronger.

_____ The sun heats the ground. Columns of hot air rise where the ground is the hottest.

_____ This process speeds up and increases. It generates extremely high winds.

2 Tornadoes occur mostly in the United States. If possible, work with a partner from your country. What kinds of severe weather (for example, hurricanes, typhoons, floods, blizzards) happen in your country? Make a list. Then write it on the board. As a class, make a chart of the different kinds of severe weather in each country.

Country	Kinds of Severe Weather

3 It is important to be able to predict tornadoes in order to save lives. What other occurrences is it important to be able to predict? Work with two or three classmates. Make a list. Compare it with your other classmates' lists.

Crossword Puzzle

Read the clues on the next page. Write the answers in the correct spaces in the puzzle.

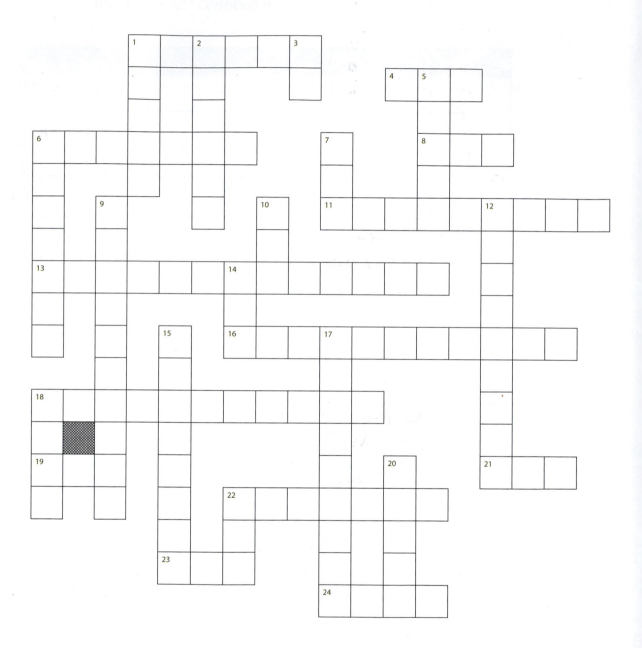

Crossword Puzzle Clues

ACROSS CLUES

1. Nexrad is a weather predicting _____ in the United States.
4. We _____ studying English.
6. We enjoy warm, sunny _____ .
8. The past tense of **do**
11. The number of deaths from plane accidents has _____ recently. That's good news!
13. Modern technology is an _____ part of our lives. We cannot live and work without it.
16. Severe storms can be very _____ . They flatten buildings and kill people.
18. Weather _____ are people who try to predict storms and other bad weather.
19. Every; each
21. The opposite of **no**
22. Many people try to _____ the future. They try to tell what will happen.
23. The present tense of **ate**
24. I am _____ that it will rain tomorrow. I am certain.

DOWN CLUES

1. New York is a _____ in the United States. California is, too.
2. Nexrad is shaped like a _____ . The Earth and the moon are this shape, too.
3. I, _____ ; he, him; she, her; we, us
5. Nexrad means "Next Generation Weather _____ ."
6. We heard a _____ on the radio that a severe thunderstorm is coming.
7. The past tense of **have**
9. _____ , most people don't work on Saturday and Sunday in the United States.
10. John _____ speak two languages.
12. An airplane crashed in the mountains last night. _____ , no one was killed.
14. We are coming to the _____ of this book. The next chapter is the last chapter.
15. Nexrad is very _____ , or correct.
17. _____ are very powerful; they can destroy trees and buildings in a few minutes.
18. After a severe storm, some areas may be completely _____ because the buildings were destroyed.
20. Certain types of storms _____ only in particular parts of the world.
22. The past tense of **put**

Cloze Quiz

Read the following paragraphs. Fill in the blanks with the correct words from the list. Use each word only once.

ahead	eyewitness	prepare	warning
characteristics	obsolete	result	
decreased	predict	severe	

Nexrad can detect strong winds and rain, which are _characteristics_ (1) of severe thunderstorms and tornadoes. In the past, a now-_obsolete_ (2) radar system was used to predict such storms. Under this old system, warnings often depended on _eyewitness_ (3) reports. These reports gave people only about three minutes to _prepare_ (4) for the tornado.

Today, there are 159 Nexrad systems in the United States. In the past, many _severe_ (5) thunderstorms and tornadoes struck without _warning_ (6) . Weather forecasters could not _predict_ (7) all of them. Now, Nexrad predicts more than 60 percent of all tornadoes. Because of this, weather forecasters can tell people _ahead_ (8) of time so that they can prepare for a tornado. As a _result_ (9) , the number of people who die in tornadoes in the U.S. _decreased_ (10) by 50 percent. In other words, this number was cut in half!

accurately	hour	only	weather
all	indispensable	several	
destructive	occur	tornado	

Tornadoes _____occur_____ (11) all over the world, but most often in the United States. One-third of _____all_____ (12) U.S. tornadoes strike in Oklahoma, Texas, and Kansas. Alaska is the _____only_____ (13) state that has never had a _____tornado_____ (14). A tornado may last from several seconds to _____several_____ (15) hours, and its winds may reach up to 300 miles per _____hour_____ (16) (500 kilometers per hour). Because tornadoes are so powerful and so _____destructive_____ (17), it is important to be able to predict them _____accurately_____ (18). Consequently, the Nexrad system is an _____indispensable_____ (19). part of American _____weather_____ (20) forecasting.

12
CHAPTER

Clues and Criminal Investigation

Prereading Preparation

1 What kinds of evidence can prove that a person committed a crime? Work with a partner. Look at the list of clues below and decide what type of crime these clues might help solve. Some clues may help solve more than one kind of crime. When you are finished, compare your ideas with your other classmates' ideas. Are your ideas the same?

Clues	Types of Crime
blood	
bullets	
clothing fibers	
dirt	
fingerprints	
footprints	
hair	
pieces of glass	
a ransom note	

2 Think of a crime that you heard about or read about. Describe it to your partner. What clues did the police use to help them solve this crime?

3 Read the title of this story. What do you think the reading will be about?

Reading

Directions: Read each paragraph carefully. Then answer the questions.

Clues and Criminal Investigation

If you wanted to solve a crime such as a robbery or a murder, how would you start? What types of evidence would you look for? Crime experts all have a basic principle, or belief: a criminal always brings something to the scene of a crime and always leaves something there. As a result, crime experts always begin their criminal investigation with a careful examination of the place where the crime occurred.

1 A **crime expert** is
   a. a professional at committing crimes
   b. a professional at solving crimes

2 A **principle** is
   a. an idea
   b. evidence
   c. a belief

3 What do crime experts think?
   a. They think that criminals are usually not very careful.
   b. They think that they can solve every crime that occurs.
   c. They think that they will always find clues at the scene of a crime.

4 What do you think the next paragraph will discuss?

_____

When criminal investigators arrive at the scene of a crime, they look for evidence, or clues, from the criminal. This evidence includes footprints, fingerprints, lip prints on glasses, hair, blood, clothing fibers, and bullet shells. These are all clues that the criminal may have left behind. Some clues are taken to laboratories and analyzed. For instance, fingerprints are "lifted" from a glass, a door, or a table. They are examined and compared by computer with the millions of fingerprints on file with the police, the Federal Bureau of Investigation (FBI), and other agencies.

5 The **scene of a crime** is

   a. a part of a movie

   b. the place where the crime occurred

   c. a description of the crime

6 When criminal investigators arrive at the scene of a crime, they look for **evidence,** or clues, from the criminal.

   a. **Evidence** means

     1. clues

     2. criminals

     3. beliefs

   b. Some examples of clues are

   _____

   _____

7 Fingerprints are **"lifted"** from a glass, a door, or a table. Then experts analyze them in a laboratory.

   In this sentence, **lifted** means

   a. found

   b. taken

   c. examined

8 What do you think the next part of this story will discuss?

   _____

In the case of murder, experts examine blood and compare it to the blood of the victim. If the blood isn't the victim's, then it might be the murderer's. Furthermore, experts can analyze the DNA from a person's cells, such as skin cells. Like fingerprints, each person's DNA is unique, which means that everyone's DNA is different. These clues help to identify the criminal.

In some cases, a criminal uses a gun when committing a crime. Every gun leaves distinctive marks on a bullet when the gun is fired. The police may find a bullet at the scene or recover a bullet from a victim's body. Experts can examine the markings on the bullet and prove that it was fired from a specific gun. This clue is strong evidence that the owner of the gun may be guilty. Consequently, the police will suspect that this person committed the crime.

9 In the case of murder, experts examine blood and compare it to the blood of the **victim.**

A **victim** is

a. the person who committed the crime
b. the person the crime is committed against

10 **Furthermore,** experts can analyze the DNA from a person's cells, such as skin cells.

Furthermore means

a. in addition
b. farther away
c. however

11 **Like fingerprints, each person's DNA is unique, which means that everyone's DNA is different.**

a. **Unique** means

1. from a person's body
2. original; individual
3. special

b. Which one of the following sentences is true?

1. Each person's DNA and fingerprints are different from every other person's.
2. Each person's DNA is different from every other person's, but their fingerprints are not.
3. Each person's fingerprints are different from every other person's, but their DNA is not.

12 **a.** Every gun leaves **distinctive** marks on a bullet when the gun is fired. **Distinctive** means

   1. particular; unique
   2. thick; heavy
   3. straight; lined

  b. The markings on bullets fired from two different guns

   1. can sometimes be the same
   2. can never be the same

13 A gun's **owner** is

  a. the person who used the gun
  b. the person that the gun belongs to
  c. the person who found the gun

14 **a.** **The police suspect that a person has committed a crime.** This sentence means that

   1. the police are sure that a specific person has committed a crime
   2. the police believe that a specific person has committed a crime

  b. **Suspect** means

   1. think that something is true
   2. know that something is true

15 **Consequently**, the police will suspect that this person committed the crime.

Consequently means

  a. in addition
  b. however
  c. as a result

Clues from the scene of a crime help the police identify a suspect. If other evidence supports these clues, then the police can charge the suspect with the crime. It is important to remember, however, that in the United States, a person is innocent until proven guilty in a court of law.

16 The police charge a person with a crime when
   a. they find a gun that belongs to that person
   b. they have blood and bullets from the scene of the crime
   c. they have evidence to show that the person may have committed the crime

17 a. The words **innocent** and **guilty**
   1. have the opposite meaning
   2. have the same meaning

   b. An **innocent** person
   1. committed a crime
   2. did not commit a crime

   c. A **guilty** person
   1. committed a crime
   2. did not commit a crime

Directions: Now read the complete passage. When you are finished, answer the questions that follow.

Clues and Criminal Investigation

1   If you wanted to solve a crime such as a robbery or a murder, how would
2   you start? What types of evidence would you look for? Crime experts all have
3   a basic principle, or belief: a criminal always brings something to the scene of
4   a crime and always leaves something there. As a result, crime experts always
5   begin their criminal investigation with a careful examination of the place where
6   the crime occurred.

7   When criminal investigators arrive at the scene of a crime, they look for
8   evidence, or clues, from the criminal. This evidence includes footprints,
9   fingerprints, lip prints on glasses, hair, blood, clothing fibers, and bullet
10 shells. These are all clues that the criminal may have left behind. Some clues
11 are taken to laboratories and analyzed. For instance, fingerprints are "lifted"
12 from a glass, a door, or a table. They are examined and compared by computer
13 with the millions of fingerprints on file with the police, the Federal Bureau of
14 Investigation (FBI), and other agencies.

15 In the case of murder, experts examine blood and compare it to the blood
16 of the victim. If the blood isn't the victim's, then it might be the murderer's.
17 Furthermore, experts can analyze the DNA from a person's cells, such as
18 skin cells. Like fingerprints, each person's DNA is unique, which means that
19 everyone's DNA is different. These clues help to identify the criminal.

20 In some cases, a criminal uses a gun when committing a crime. Every gun
21 leaves distinctive marks on a bullet when the gun is fired. The police may find a
22 bullet at the scene or recover a bullet from a victim's body. Experts can examine
23 the markings on the bullet and prove that it was fired from a specific gun. This
24 clue is strong evidence that the owner of the gun may be guilty. Consequently,
25 the police will suspect that this person committed the crime.

26 Clues from the scene of a crime help the police identify a suspect. If other
27 evidence supports these clues, then the police can charge the suspect with the
28 crime. It is important to remember, however, that in the United States, a person
29 is innocent until proven guilty in a court of law.

Scanning for Information

Read the questions. Then go back to the complete passage and scan quickly for the answers. Circle the letter of the correct answer, or write your answer.

1 What do all crime experts believe?

_____

_____

2 Why are fingerprints from the scene of a crime compared with the fingerprints on file with the police, the FBI, and other agencies?

_____

_____

3 If the blood found at the scene of a murder isn't the victim's blood, why might it be the murderer's blood?

_____

_____

4 Why are blood, skin, and fingerprints so important to crime experts?

_____

_____

5 What is the main idea of this story?
   a. Criminals often leave clues at the scene of a crime.
   b. Fingerprints and bullets are important evidence of crimes.
   c. Crime experts analyze a variety of clues to identify criminals.

Word Forms

In English, some nouns (n.) become adjectives (adj.) by adding *-ful*. Read the sentences below. Decide if each sentence needs a noun (n.) or an adjective (adj.). Circle the correct answer.

1 Criminal investigators are very <u>skill / skillful</u>.
                                (n.)   (adj.)

2 Their <u>skill / skillful</u> is very important in helping them solve crimes.
      (n.)   (adj.)

3 Roseanne gave her elderly father a lot of <u>help / helpful</u> when he was sick.
                                                      (n.)   (adj.)

4 Because Roseanne was so <u>help / helpful</u> to her father, he felt better quickly.
                            (n.)   (adj.)

5 Jerry is always very <u>care / careful</u> when he paints his house.
                    (n.)   (adj.)

6 He takes a lot of <u>care / careful</u> not to spill paint on the carpets.
                  (n.)   (adj.)

7 Gilda is unusually <u>success / successful</u> in her career.
                 (n.)   (adj.)

8 She achieved <u>success / successful</u> in only a few years.
             (n.)   (adj.)

Word Partnership	Use *success* with
n.	success **of a business,** **chance for/of** success, success **or failure,** **key to** success, **lack of** success
v.	**achieve** success, success **depends on** *something*, **enjoy** success
adj.	**great** success, **huge** success, **recent** success, **tremendous** success

Vocabulary in Context

Read the sentences. Choose the correct word for each sentence. Write your answers on the blank lines.

| evidence *(n.)* | expert *(n.)* | principle *(n.)* | suspect *(n.)* |

1 Emily is the most likely _____ in the murder of her husband. The police think she may have killed him.

2 Sam is a police _____ on guns and rifles. He knows more about these weapons than anyone else in the police department.

3 A strong _____ in American law is that a person is considered innocent until proven guilty.

4 The police suspect that Jean committed the store robbery, but they don't have any _____ against her, so they have to let her go.

| consequently *(adv.)* | furthermore *(adv.)* | if *(conj.)* |

5 I would go on vacation _____ I had enough money, but I don't. Perhaps I'll take a vacation next year.

6 An eyewitness saw John steal a car. The police found the stolen car in John's garage. _____ , the police arrested John and charged him with the crime.

7 I'm sure that Nelson didn't shoot Tom. Nelson and Tom are very good friends. Someone else's fingerprints were on the gun. _____ , Nelson was out of town on business when Tom was shot.

| investigated *(v.)* | occurred *(v.)* | suspected *(v.)* |

8 Ten murders _____ in Johnston City last year.

9 When the FBI _____ the bank robbery, they found out that the robbers had left the country.

10 Everyone _____ that Fran stole the money, but no one was able to prove it.

D

Topics for Discussion and Writing

1 Work in a small group. Find a story about a crime in a book, magazine, or newspaper. Read the description of the crime, the clues, and the suspect. Decide if the suspect is guilty and write a paragraph explaining your opinion. Present your case to the class.

2 What do you think is the most important kind of evidence at a crime scene? Why is this evidence the most important? Write a paragraph. Explain your opinion.

3 Many people enjoy watching TV programs about crimes and criminal investigations. Do you enjoy watching these kinds of shows? Why or why not? Why do you think these shows are popular? Discuss your reasons with your classmates.

4 **Write in your journal.** Think about a crime you read or heard about. Describe the crime. What happened? When and where did this crime take place? How did the police investigate it? What clues did they find? How did they solve the crime? Share your story with a classmate. Which crime was more difficult to solve? Why?

Follow-up Activities

1 Work with two or three partners. Imagine that you are a group of crime experts. The police have asked you to investigate the following crimes. What clues will you look for at the scene of each crime? What additional evidence will you try to get in order to identify a suspect for each of these crimes? Complete the chart.

Type of Crime	Clues at the Scene of the Crime	Additional Evidence
a murder		
a kidnapping		
a house break-in		
a jewelry store robbery		

2 Work with one or two partners. Make up a crime and write a list of some evidence to leave "at the scene of the crime." Then have your classmates investigate your crime and try to solve it. When you have all finished, discuss your evidence. Which group had the best clues?

UNIT 6   FUTURE TECHNOLOGY TODAY

F Crossword Puzzle

Read the clues on the next page. Write the answers in the correct spaces in the puzzle.

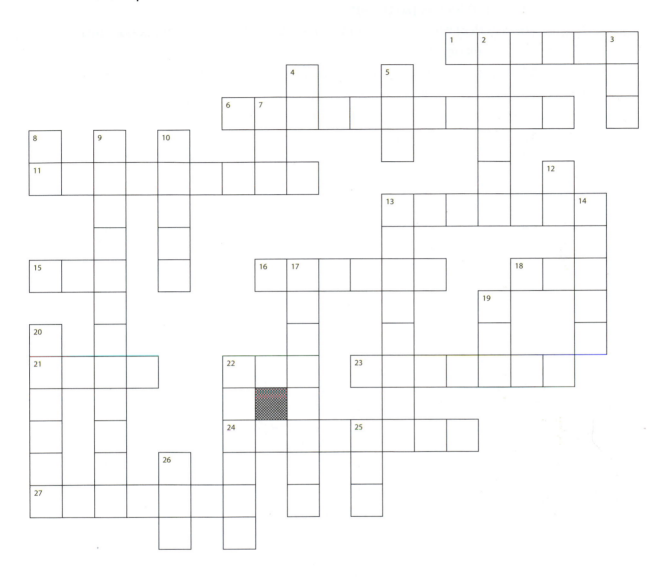

Crossword Puzzle Clues

1. A gun leaves particular markings on a _____ .
6. My dog has _____ markings. He has a black leg, a black ear, and a black spot on his head.
11. I have a very simple _____ , or belief: I try my best with everything I do.
13. The police may ask many different _____ for help to solve a crime: chemists, dentists, etc.
15. We _____ doing a crossword puzzle.
16. John was the _____ of a robbery yesterday. Someone robbed him on the street.
18. Each; every
21. Uncommon; unusual
22. The past tense of **get**
23. Experts can _____ blood, hair, clothing, and other clues to a crime.
24. Mary did not steal John's wallet. She is _____ of that crime.
27. The police have a _____ in yesterday's bank robbery. They think they know who did it.

2. Everyone's fingerprints are _____ . No two people have the same fingerprints.
3. Maria is studying English, and we are, _____ .
4. Robert is _____ tall as Gary. They are the same height.
5. Each person's _____ is unique, just like his or her fingerprints.
7. Sick; not well
8. The opposite of **down**
9. The lines on a person's fingers are _____ .
10. Crimes _____ , or take place, every day.
12. Our class ends _____ 10 o'clock.
13. The police don't have any _____ , or clues, in this case yet.
14. Many specialists help the police _____ crimes.
17. The police look for clues, for _____ , blood, hair, bullets, fingerprints.
19. The present tense of **said**
20. Murder, robbery, kidnapping, and car theft are all types of _____ .
22. Tom was found _____ of stealing cars. The evidence against him was very strong.
25. We _____ do crossword puzzles.
26. The past tense of **let**

Cloze Quiz

Read the following paragraphs. Fill in the blanks with the correct words from the list. Use each word only once.

belief	crime	leaves	start
careful	evidence	occurred	
case	furthermore	result	

If you wanted to solve a _____ such as a robbery
(1)

or a murder, how would you _____? What types of
(2)

_____ would you look for? Crime experts all have a basic
(3)

principle, or _____: a criminal always brings something to
(4)

the scene of a crime and always _____ something there. As a
(5)

_____, crime experts always begin their criminal investigation
(6)

with a _____ examination of the place where the crime
(7)

_____. In the _____ of murder, experts examine
(8)   (9)

blood and compare it to the blood of the victim. _____, experts
(10)

can analyze the DNA from a person's cells, such as skin cells.

bullet	experts	scene	uses
clues	guilty	specific	
consequently	gun	suspect	

In some cases, a criminal _____ a gun when
(11)

committing a crime. Every gun leaves distinctive marks on a bullet

when the _____ is fired. The police may find a bullet
(12)

at the _____ , or recover a bullet from a victim's body.
(13)

_____ can examine the markings on the _____
(14)   (15)

and prove that it was fired from a _____ gun. This clue is
(16)

strong evidence that the owner of the gun may be guilty. _____ ,
(17)

the police will _____ that this person committed the crime.
(18)

All these clues may help police identify a suspect. If other evidence supports

these _____ , then the police can charge the suspect with the
(19)

crime. It is important to remember, however, that in the United States, a

person is innocent until proven _____ in a court of law.
(20)

INDEX OF KEY WORDS AND PHRASES

Words in blue are on the Academic Word List (AWL), Coxhead (2000). The AWL is a list of the 570 highest-frequency academic word families that regularly appear in academic texts. The list was compiled by researcher Averil Coxhead from a corpus of 3.5 million words.

A

accomplishments 6, 8
accurately 159, 161
achievements 7, 8
active 65, 66, 67, 68, 69
afraid 111, 114
agencies 174, 178
alone 38, 40
already 66, 68, 142, 144
although 80, 82
amazingly 157, 161
Americans 18, 19, 21, 22, 23
analyze 174, 175, 178
anthropologist 95, 98
anthropology 95, 96, 97, 99
anywhere else 18, 22
Arctic 141, 142, 143
as a result 97, 99, 157, 158, 161, 173, 178
assist 109, 113
astronauts 125, 129
at first 109, 111, 114
at least 65, 68, 79, 82
at that time 108, 113
attacked 108, 113

B

backwards 80, 82
baseball 65, 68
basketball 65, 68
because of 98, 99, 111, 114, 140, 143, 159, 161
belief 173, 178
benefit 112, 114
billion 126, 128, 129
bored 52, 53
boroughs 80, 82
both 95, 98
brief 126, 129

C

cancer 80, 82
carefully 109, 114
cause 111, 112, 114
characteristic 158, 161
charge 177, 178
cheered 79, 82
chemist 109, 113
cholesterol 66, 68
city dwellers 19, 22
climbing ropes 67, 69
clues 173, 174, 175, 177, 178
comfortable 5, 7, 8

common 95, 99
communicating 5, 8
conditions 66, 68
confidence 7, 8
correct 125, 129
cough syrup 109, 113
countryside 19, 22
crime 173, 174, 175, 177, 178
criminal 173, 174, 175, 178
culture 95, 96, 97, 99
cure 108, 111, 113, 114
curious 109, 113
customers 109, 113

D

deadly 108, 113
decide 39, 40, 51, 52, 53, 95, 96, 99, 109, 113
decrease 140, 141, 143, 159, 161
depend 158, 161
destroyed 157, 161
destructive 159, 161
detect 158, 161
developed 112, 114, 125, 129
devised 112, 114
diapers 38, 40
diary 5, 7
diet 67, 68
difficult 6, 8
disease 108, 111, 112, 113, 114
distinctive 175, 178
district 157, 161
DNA 175, 178
dress 38, 39, 40
druggists 109, 113
dweller 19, 22

E

encouragement 79, 82
enjoy 7, 8, 51, 52, 53, 109, 113
especially 96, 99, 109, 113
events 80, 82
evidence 173, 174, 175, 177, 178
excitement 80, 82
exercise 65, 66, 67, 68, 69
experts 173, 175, 178
expressing 5, 7
eyewitness 158, 161

F

famous 95, 97, 98, 99
far 125, 129
feed 38, 39, 40

few 79, 80, 82, 141, 144, 158, 161
fibers 174, 178
fingerprints 174, 175, 178
fitness 66, 68
flattened 157, 161
footprints 174, 178
for example 5, 7, 19, 21, 22, 66, 68, 80, 82, 111, 114, 142, 144
for instance 20, 22, 174, 178
forecasters 158, 159, 161
forecasting 157, 159, 161
formed 126, 129
founder 80, 82
furthermore 175, 178

G

germs 111, 112, 114
global warming 141, 143
gradually 5, 8
guess 125, 129
guilty 175, 177, 178

H

habits 67, 69
happy 18, 19, 21, 22, 23
health 66, 67, 68, 69
high blood pressure 66, 68
homeschool 51, 53
homeschooling 39, 40
hometown 18, 19, 21, 22, 23
however 18, 19, 22, 79, 80, 82, 126, 129, 140, 142, 143, 144, 177, 178
huge 126, 129

I

ice cap 141, 143
identify 175, 177, 178
ill 80, 82, 108, 111, 113, 114
impact 126, 128, 129
improve 51, 53
in addition 5, 7
in contrast 66, 68
in fact 18, 22, 37, 40, 52, 53, 66, 68, 79, 82, 109, 111, 114
in other words 4, 7, 159, 161
inactivity 66, 68
indispensable 159, 161
innocent 177, 178
inoculation 111, 114
instead of 80, 82
intelligent 109, 114
interested 95, 97, 99, 109, 113
investigators 174, 178

Iowa 37, 40
iron 126, 129

J
journal 5, 6, 7, 8
jumping 67, 69

K
kindergarten 66, 68

L
laboratories 174, 178
lessons 6, 8, 52, 53
lifetime 112, 114
limit 79, 82
location 19, 22

M
marathon 79, 80, 82
marks 175, 178
Mars 126, 129
massive 157, 161
materials 126, 129
medicine 109, 112, 113, 114
method 111, 114
modern 108, 109, 112, 113, 114, 158, 161
move 19, 23, 51, 53
movement 125, 129
musical instrument 52, 53

N
natural 4, 7
neighbors 21, 23
Nexrad 158, 159, 161
Northeast Passage 140, 141, 142, 143, 144

O
object 126, 129
observations 111, 114
obsolete 158, 161
occur 158, 161, 173, 178
of course 20, 22
offered 79, 82
on the other hand 21, 23
orbit 126, 129
ordinarily 157, 161
origin 125, 129
outer 126, 129
overweight 66, 68

P
participants 79, 80, 82
pasteurization 112, 114
patient 4, 7, 111, 114
peaceful 96, 99
perform 52, 53
perhaps 6, 8, 108, 113, 126, 129
pharmacists 109, 113
physical education 66, 68
pieces 125, 126, 129
pills 109, 113
popular 39, 40, 79, 82, 97, 99
positive 4, 7, 8
powerful 159, 161
predict 158, 159, 161
prefer 19, 20, 21, 22, 23
prevent 112, 114
principle 173, 178
process 112, 114
prove 125, 128, 129, 175, 177, 178

Q
quiet 21, 23, 52, 53

R
rabies 108, 111, 113, 114
race 79, 80, 82
radar 158, 161
recently 79, 82
record 6, 7, 8
recover 175, 178
remarkable 97, 99
roller hockey 65, 68
route 140, 142 143, 144
running 67, 69, 80, 82
rural area 19, 22

S
Samoa 96, 97, 99
Samoan 96, 97, 99
scene 173, 174, 175, 177, 178
septuplets 37, 38, 39, 40
serious 111, 114
several 3, 5, 7, 141, 142, 143, 144, 159, 161
severe 158, 159, 161
shortcut 141, 143
shot 111, 114
shrinking 141, 143

sick 108, 113
slowly 80, 82, 109, 111, 114
solve 173, 178
somewhere else 19, 21, 22, 23
specific 175, 178
sphere 158, 161
spoil 111, 112, 114
sports 66, 67, 68, 69
step 4, 5, 6, 7, 8
subject 97, 99
support 128, 129, 175, 178
suspect 175, 177, 178
systems 158, 159, 161

T
team 65, 67, 68, 69
technology 158, 161
teenage 96, 99
theory 126, 128, 129
therefore 66, 68
thoughtful 109, 114
throw away 51, 53
thunderstorm 158, 159, 161
together 37, 40, 50, 52, 53, 126, 129
too 20, 22, 38, 40, 51, 53, 80, 82, 95, 96, 98, 99, 109, 113, 141, 142, 143, 144
tornado 157, 158, 159, 161
traditionally 142, 143
travel 95, 97, 99, 140, 142, 143
treat 111, 114
types 109, 113, 173, 178

U
unhealthy 66, 68
unimportant 79, 82
unique 175, 178
until 97, 99, 177, 178
unusual 37, 40, 80, 82, 95, 99

V
vaccination 111, 112, 114
victim 175, 178
video games 50, 51, 53

W
warn 158, 161
warning 158, 161
whole 80, 82
wondered 125, 129

SKILLS INDEX

GRAMMAR AND USAGE

Word forms
- Adjectives that become adverbs by adding -*ly*, 9–10
- Adjectives that become nouns by adding -*ness*, 25–26
- Nouns that become adjectives by adding -*ful*, 180
- Verbs that become nouns by adding -*ence* or -*ance*, 100–101, 163
- Verbs that become nouns by adding -*ment*, 84
- Verbs that become nouns by adding -*tion*, 131–132
- Verbs that become nouns by dropping the final -*e* and adding -*tion*, 115–116
- Words that can be either nouns or verbs, 41–42, 55, 70–71, 146

Word partnerships, 10, 26, 42, 55, 71, 84, 101, 116, 132, 146, 163, 180

LISTENING/SPEAKING

- Asking/answering questions, 30
- Discussion, 13, 17, 28, 30, 44, 64, 73, 74, 86, 102, 103, 107, 118, 119, 134, 148, 172, 182, 184
- Group activities, 13, 17, 28, 30, 44, 73, 74, 86, 118, 119, 134, 148, 182, 184
- Interviewing, 103
- Partner activities, 13, 28, 64, 102, 107, 172, 173
- Reporting, 13, 182

READING

- Charts, 29, 30, 87, 88
- Comprehension, 3–7, 18–22, 37–39, 50–52, 65–68, 79–81, 95–98, 108–113, 125–128, 140–143, 157–160, 173–177
- Descriptions, 102, 182
- Follow-up activities, 13, 29–30, 45, 58, 74, 87–88, 103, 119, 134, 149, 166–167, 183–184
- Lists, 13, 172
- Prereading preparation, 2–3, 17, 49, 64, 78, 94–95, 107, 124, 153, 156, 172–173
- Scanning for information, 8–9, 24, 41, 54, 69–70, 83, 99–100, 115, 130–131, 145, 162, 179
- Vocabulary in context, 10–11, 26–27, 43–44, 56–57, 71–72, 85–86, 101–102, 117–118, 132–133, 147–148, 164–165, 181–182

TEST-TAKING SKILLS

- Cloze quizzes, 16, 33, 48, 61, 91, 106, 122, 137–138, 152–153, 170–171, 187–188
- Fill in blanks, 10–11, 26–27, 43–44, 56–57, 71–72, 85–86, 88, 132–133, 147–148, 149, 164–165, 181–182
- Multiple-choice questions, 3–7, 8, 9, 17, 18–20, 21–22, 24, 29, 36, 37, 38–39, 41, 50–51, 52, 54, 64, 65, 66–68, 70, 79–80, 81, 83, 94, 95, 96, 97–98, 100, 107, 108–110, 111–113, 115, 125–127, 128, 130, 131, 140–142, 143, 153, 157, 158–159, 160, 162, 173, 174, 175–177, 179
- Putting items in order, 166

Short-answer questions, 8–9, 20, 21, 24, 29, 37, 39, 41, 50, 51, 52, 54, 65, 66, 69–70, 83, 96, 97, 99–100, 108, 110, 111, 112, 115, 126, 130–131, 140, 142, 145, 149, 153, 158, 162, 173, 174, 179

True/false questions, 3, 6, 18, 20, 21, 37, 38, 50, 51, 66, 67, 68, 79, 80–81, 95, 96, 110–111, 125, 126, 128, 157, 158, 159

Yes/no questions, 87, 140

TOPICS

Cabey-Gray family, 49–60
Clues and criminal investigation, 172–188
Exercise for children, 64–77
Learning a second language, 2–16
Louis Pasteur, 107–122
Maps, 139–153
Margaret Mead, 94–106
McCaughey Family, 36–48
New York City Marathon, 78–93
Origin of the moon, 124–138
The best place to live, 17–33
Weather forecasting, 156–171

VIEWING

Maps, 149, 153
Photographs, 17, 36, 49, 64, 78, 94, 107, 156

WRITING

Charts, 13, 17, 30, 36, 45, 49, 58, 64, 74, 119, 124, 167, 183
Crossword puzzles, 14–15, 31–32, 46–47, 59–60, 75–76, 89–90, 104–105, 120–121, 135–137, 150–151, 168–169, 185–186
Descriptions, 73, 95, 102, 118, 165, 182
Discussion, 103
Examples, 102
Explanations, 12, 28, 57, 102, 118, 134, 182
Group activities, 45, 58, 74, 78, 103, 119, 124, 134, 167, 182, 183
Journals, 1–3, 12, 28, 44, 57, 73, 86, 118, 134, 148, 165, 182
Letters, 12, 73, 86, 134
Lists, 2–3, 28, 45, 74, 78, 119, 134, 165, 167, 172
Paragraphs, 57, 102, 118, 134, 165, 182
Partner activities, 2–3, 17, 28, 36, 44, 58, 64, 165, 167
Plans, 73, 134
Reasons, 17
Schedules, 44
Sentences, 95